THE BEDFORD SERIES IN HISTORY AND CULTURE

The Influenza Pandemic of 1918–1919

A Brief History with Documents

Susan Kingsley Kent

University of Colorado, Boulder

BEDFORD / ST. MARTIN'S Boston ◆ New York

For Bedford/St. Martin's

Publisher for History: Mary V. Dougherty
Executive Editor for History: Traci M. Crowell
Director of Development for History: Jane Knetzger
Senior Editor: Heidi L. Hood
Developmental Editor: Ann Kirby-Payne
Production Supervisor: Lisa Chow
Executive Marketing Manager: Jenna Bookin Barry
Editorial Assistant: Laura Kintz
Project Management: Books By Design, Inc.
Cartography: Mapping Specialists, Ltd.
Permissions Manager: Kalina K. Ingham
Text Designer: Claire Seng-Niemoeller
Cover Designer: Marine Miller
Cover Photo: Japanese schoolgirls wear protective masks to guard against the influenza outbreak in Tokyo, February 17, 1920. © Bettmann/Getty Images
Composition: Achorn International, Inc.
Printing and Binding: RR Donnelley and Sons

President, Bedford/St. Martin's: Denise B. Wydra
Presidents, Macmillan Higher Education: Joan E. Feinberg and Tom Scotty
Director of Marketing: Karen R. Soeltz
Director of Production: Susan W. Brown
Associate Production Director: Elise S. Kaiser
Manager, Publishing Services: Andrea Cava

Library of Congress Control Number: 2012939219

Manufactured in the United States of America.

7 6 5 4 3 2
f e d c b a

For information, write: Bedford/St. Martin's, 75 Arlington Street, Boston, MA 02116 (617-399-4000)

ISBN: 978-0-312-67708-4

Acknowledgments

Acknowledgments and copyrights are continued at the back of the book on page 125, which constitutes an extension of the copyright page. It is a violation of the law to reproduce these selections by any means whatsoever without the written permission of the copyright holder.

Foreword

The Bedford Series in History and Culture is designed so that readers can study the past as historians do.

The historian's first task is finding the evidence. Documents, letters, memoirs, interviews, pictures, movies, novels, or poems can provide facts and clues. Then the historian questions and compares the sources. There is more to do than in a courtroom, for hearsay evidence is welcome, and the historian is usually looking for answers beyond act and motive. Different views of an event may be as important as a single verdict. How a story is told may yield as much information as what it says.

Along the way the historian seeks help from other historians and perhaps from specialists in other disciplines. Finally, it is time to write, to decide on an interpretation and how to arrange the evidence for readers.

Each book in this series contains an important historical document or group of documents, each document a witness from the past and open to interpretation in different ways. The documents are combined with some element of historical narrative—an introduction or a biographical essay, for example—that provides students with an analysis of the primary source material and important background information about the world in which it was produced.

Each book in the series focuses on a specific topic within a specific historical period. Each provides a basis for lively thought and discussion about several aspects of the topic and the historian's role. Each is short enough (and inexpensive enough) to be a reasonable one-week assignment in a college course. Whether as classroom or personal reading, each book in the series provides firsthand experience of the challenge—and fun—of discovering, recreating, and interpreting the past.

Lynn Hunt
David W. Blight
Bonnie G. Smith
Natalie Zemon Davis

Preface

Appearing in the midst of the First World War, the influenza virus of 1918–1919 blazed across the globe in a matter of months, leaving in its wake a death toll that would surpass that of the war itself. It appeared suddenly and with explosive impact, and defied all previous understandings of the disease: the illness struck quickly and without warning, felling people in their homes, at work, and in the streets, and unlike previous manifestations of the disease, which tended to take infants and the elderly, this strain primarily struck men and women in the prime of their lives. Especially virulent, it moved quickly through homes, military barracks, cities, and towns, first appearing in the American Midwest and quickly making its way to South America, Africa, Europe, Asia, and Australia. Doctors and other medical professionals were helpless to understand or treat it, and governments were unable to contain or manage it. By the time the virus died out in the fall of 1919, it had taken the lives of up to sixty million people. Like the war, the pandemic shook the foundations of individuals, families, and entire societies around the globe, and its impact would continue to be felt throughout the first half of the twentieth century.

Despite its global impact, the pandemic is basically unknown to many students today. Designed for students enrolled in a variety of courses from surveys of global history to courses on health and medicine, World War I and beyond, this accessible and engaging collection invites critical thought on the connections between public health, economics, politics, and historical events.

The introduction to the volume provides a compelling, brief overview of the pandemic, including a thorough description of its physical symptoms and an examination of how and where it spread, as well as insights into the medical community's understanding of—and response to—the disease. The short- and long-term impacts of the pandemic—from the lives of children orphaned by the flu to colonial rebellions for which the pandemic served as a major catalyst—are also discussed.

The introduction is supported by more than sixty documents organized in four sections: The Nature and Experience of the Disease; Transmission and Mortality; Treatment Responses; and Consequences and Repercussions of the Pandemic. The documents include firsthand accounts from doctors and nurses who struggled to cope with this new strain of influenza while they treated patients ranging from anonymous rural Japanese villagers to the President of the United States. Along with newspaper accounts, government notices and statistical surveys, and memoirs and novels written by survivors, this collection of primary sources offers a glimpse into the experience of the pandemic as it unfolded, as well as its impact on individuals, communities, and entire populations in the decades that followed. To illustrate the truly global nature of the disease, the sources report on experiences from a wide range of countries, including the United States, Ireland, South Africa, Sweden, India, Nigeria, China, Sierra Leone, Germany, and beyond. Illuminating headnotes and gloss notes provide necessary context and background, while a chronology of events, questions for consideration, and a selected bibliography enhance and enrich student understanding.

ACKNOWLEDGMENTS

Many people contributed to the creation of this volume, and I am pleased to be able to thank them for their ideas, criticisms, suggestions, and assistance in putting it together. My dear friend Bonnie Smith got me involved in this project in the first place, for which I am most grateful. The editorial staff at Bedford/St. Martin's—Mary Dougherty, Traci Mueller Crowell, Heidi Hood, Laura Kintz, and Andrea Cava—provided extensive hands-on help at every stage of the process. They are a warm, friendly, thoughtful, and professional bunch of people, and I enjoyed working with them tremendously. Nancy Benjamin at Books By Design carefully managed the day-to-day production work and made useful changes as copy editor. Ann Kirby-Payne, development editor extraordinaire, did so much to make this book work that the title of editor does not do her justice. She has been a wonderful collaborator, and I am deeply indebted to her for all the effort and creativity she put into the project.

The external readers of the manuscript provided corrections and offered criticisms that made this a far better book than it would have been otherwise; I very much appreciate their input. Among others, I particularly wish to thank Alfred W. Crosby, University of Texas at

Austin; George Fascik, Miami University, Ohio; and Nancy Fitch, California State University, Fullerton. I'd also like to thank my friend and colleague, Carol Byerly, for her generous comments and suggestions. Her own work on the 1918–1919 flu pandemic has played a crucial role in my understanding of the event; I dedicate this book to her.

Susan Kingsley Kent

Contents

Maps and Illustrations

PART ONE

Introduction: "There Was No Stopping It"

The influenza pandemic of 1918–1919 killed at least thirty million and perhaps as many as one hundred million people throughout the world.[1] Appearing in the midst of the Great War, it proved to be more deadly than any other disease since the visitations of the Black Death in the fourteenth century, and it killed more people than would any other single event of the twentieth century except World War II. George Newman, Chief Medical Officer of Great Britain's Ministry of Health in 1918, called it "one of the great historic scourges of our time, a pestilence which affected the well-being of millions of men and women and destroyed more human lives in a few months than did the European war in five years." It appeared with explosive suddenness, and "simply had its way. It came like a thief in the night and stole treasure."[2] Doctors estimated that eight hundred out of one thousand persons who came down with the flu contracted only a mild case; but some 80 percent of the other two hundred severely afflicted died.[3] In the words of one Japanese physician who struggled to treat patients in a flu-ravaged community in rural Japan at the height of the pandemic, "There was no stopping it."[4]

A FAMILIAR, YET UNPRECEDENTED ILLNESS

Like all influenza viruses, the strain of 1918–1919 spread easily. It was passed from one person to another in droplets released into the air through coughing, sneezing, and even talking. It also spread through contact: Those infected, having touched their own eyes, noses, or mouths, passed the virus to others via the objects and surfaces they touched. People who contracted the flu were contagious—that is, they could pass it along—for as much as a full day before they suffered symptoms and remained contagious for another five to seven days after they started to show signs of the illness. Environments with large concentrations of people—cities, towns, and villages, and especially military camps—enabled the virus to take hold and pass easily from one person to the next; the worldwide circulation of people and goods allowed it to move rapidly across the globe.

This strain of influenza produced in many of its victims a variety of vivid and frightening physical symptoms that had not been encountered in previous incarnations of the disease. Doctors reported some patients who "spit up a quantity of frothy sputum tinged with bright blood." "The dreaded blueness" of the face caused by heliotrope cyanosis disturbed observers—lay persons and medical professionals alike—who cited the incidence of this particular manifestation repeatedly. The "blueness" was the sign of pneumonia, of the patient's effective drowning in the fluids that had built up in the lungs.[5] The British Ministry of Health's official report on the flu included color illustrations of the shockingly purple faces of patients suffering from "this dreaded heliotrope cyanosis." This symptom signaled almost certain death, doctors came to understand. "It was amongst cases of this type that the great mortality of the epidemic occurred," observed British Ministry of Health physicians. "In going round a large ward, one could, without examining the patients at all beyond looking at their countenances, pick out those who were going to die with almost uniform certainty by reason of their colour alone."[6]

Unlike its predecessors, which tended to take infants and the elderly, this strain of influenza preferred men and women aged fifteen to forty-five, victims in the prime of their lives (Documents 4 and 48). In the United States, the flu killed men and women aged fifteen to forty-five at a rate twenty times greater than previous manifestations of the disease (see Figure 1).[7] The disease took more men than women, though pregnant women suffered particularly acutely from the illness and were the most likely to die.[8] It seems likely that the virulent nature of the virus compelled an immune response in bodies that itself served to exacerbate the severity of the illness: When bodies released toxins to fight the influenza virus—called cytokines—those toxins proved powerful enough to destroy lung tissue. In attacking the virus, in other words, the cytokines also attacked vulnerable respiratory tissue, making those possessing the strongest immune systems the most likely to succumb to respiratory illness, particularly pneumonia.[9] Medical authorities

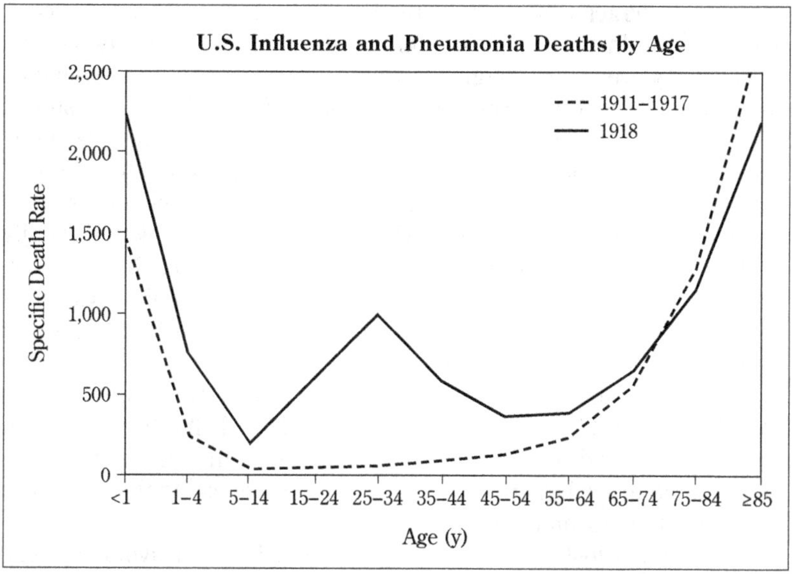

Figure 1. *The Age Distribution of Deaths from Influenza, 1911–1918*
Influenza viruses are typically most deadly for the very young and the very old, with the lowest rate of death occurring among adults in their teens, twenties, and thirties. But the 1918 virus proved markedly different, with an unprecedented death rate among adults in the prime of life. The uncharacteristic peak amongst fifteen- to forty-five-year-olds, resulting in the "terrible W" seen here, differs greatly from the more typical curve shown for 1911–1917. (Source: Taubenberger, Jeffery K., and David M. Morens. "1918 Influenza: The Mother of All Pandemics." Emerging Infectious Diseases 12.1 (2006): 15–22, Figure 2. PMC.).

could not explain this unusual characteristic of age and gender distribution of mortality, a phenomenon that contributed to the sense of utter incomprehension the disease produced within all segments of society throughout the world. This was an illness without precedent, whose etiology and treatment could not be discerned or determined.

This particular strain of influenza defied all previous understandings of the disease (Document 3). It struck quickly and without warning, felling people in their homes, in schools, in stores and businesses, and in the streets. The nature and scope of the flu compelled medical authorities to abandon their ordinarily clinical accounts and describe the situation in highly charged, graphic language. Herbert French of the British Ministry of Health recounted what he believed to be a typical situation. "In the midst of perfect health in a circumscribed community," he wrote, "such as a barracks, or a school, the first case of influenza would occur, and then within the next few hours or days a large proportion—and occasionally even every single individual of that community—would be stricken down with the same type of febrile illness, the rate of spread from one to another being remarkable. The patient would be seized rapidly, or almost suddenly, with a sense of such prostration as to be utterly unable to carry on with what he might be doing; from sheer lassitude he would be obliged to lie down where he was, or crawl with difficulty back to bed." *The Lancet,* a medical journal published in Great Britain, abandoned its scientific distance when it described the flu's "invasion of every hitherto safe nook and cranny in the inhabited world."[10] Barracks became converted to sick rooms overnight, and hospitals became so overrun with patients that they had to turn new arrivals away. Nurses and doctors could not handle the unprecedented numbers of cases; undertakers could not fill the orders for caskets that came streaming in nor could gravediggers handle the volume requesting their services (Documents 1, 10, and 11).

Some stores lost business as customers fell sick or avoided public places. One department store in Little Rock, Arkansas, noted the Arkansas *Gazette* on October 19, 1918, "which has a business of $15,000 daily, is not doing more than half that." But others saw unprecedented demand for their products: Drugstores and apothecaries couldn't keep patent medicines in stock (Document 39). As workers fell ill, labor shortages became common. Mine shutdowns in Tennessee owing to sickness reduced the production of coal there by 50 percent; some U.S. factories, already facing shortages of labor because of military conscription, reported being crippled by influenza. Public services couldn't keep pace, as transportation and utility workers became so incapacitated by illness that they could not make it to work.[11]

Combatants on the western front in Europe suffered especially harsh attacks: Laid low by fever and then by opportunistic pneumonia that took advantage of the weakened conditions of the soldiers, thousands upon thousands of them had to be invalided to the rear areas. German soldiers appeared to suffer disproportionately from the disease in June and July of 1918, experiencing great losses to illness and death (Document 51). Among the British and French forces, the first wave of the pandemic, which occurred in late spring and early summer, caused illness but not terrible disability. But the second wave, arriving in the fall, hit everyone hard: U.S. forces suffered more deaths from the flu in October 1918, at the height of their offensive against the Germans, than from battle. After the armistice in November 1918, the incidence of cases declined, but sprang back again in February of 1919. By the middle of 1919, the virus had lapsed, although it appeared again in 1920 in less lethal form.

The particular configurations of this influenza virus may have been a product of the war. The conditions of this war may well have enabled a common and usually mild disease to mutate into a deadly strain that spread like wildfire around the world, killing not only the weakest in the population but the very strongest as well. Taking advantage of thousands of people congregating together in army camps and hospitals, moving constantly in and out of contact with others, and subject to conditions in the trenches that weakened immune systems, this flu took on a character unprecedented in its impact. Flu viruses mutate regularly, but most viruses do not survive long enough for the changes to take effect. In ordinary conditions, a virus that mutated into a particularly deadly strain would not have sufficient hosts to sustain itself—it would kill off its hosts too quickly to be able to reproduce and pass on its characteristics. But the conditions of warfare in 1918 ensured that sufficient hosts—young, healthy men—were continuously made available, so that the virus could survive to reproduce. As soldiers fell ill, they were brought to the rear areas and replaced by others who rotated in to the camps and trenches. The camps and trenches were thus filled with men who had been infected with the virus but were not yet sick, on the one hand, and men who had not yet been exposed to the virus to whom they could transmit it, on the other. A steady and constant supply of noninfected troops arrived to succor the virus, ensuring that its terrible virulence was not exterminated by the elimination of its hosts. Without the particular circumstances brought on by the war, the virulent strain of influenza might not have been able to maintain its presence and take down so many victims.[12]

While the role that the war played in the spread and mutation of the virus may be debatable, there is little doubt that the two events were intertwined in people's minds, as patients and observers alike noted intimate connections between the flu and the war. For some, the war was incorporated in the hallucinations they suffered while feverish with the disease. London's *Daily Express* cited an inquest report on a nine-year-old boy whose death from the flu followed a delirious episode when he "jumped out of bed, swinging his arms about and saying he was fighting the Germans." For others, the war served as an obvious metaphor in which Germans and germs were equally to be feared. In October 1918, a British physician told an inquest panel that doctors were "fighting at home a foe as bad as the Huns." Stories about the "Influenzal Hun" who attacked innocent victims appeared in Allied newspaper accounts. An advertisement in the *Illustrated London News* warned that the flu placed Britons "under the domination of enemies more ruthless and destructive even than the Hun." The copy spoke of "'Germ-Huns' in their trenches" against whom the product touted—Kruschen Salts—"is your first line of defence." A reporter for the *Daily Express* told of his visit to a London hospital "to inspect a party of the enemy who had been taken captive . . . and were at the time interned in the 'cage' of a microscope. They wore a pink uniform," he noted. Gas masks were urged on the populace; indeed, doctors and scientists allowed as how "the lesions produced by poisonous gases during the last war resembled those seen in the respiratory complications of influenza." Although there was no such medical relationship between poison gases used in the war and influenza, some accounts suggested there was (Document 23). Doctors, asserted the *British Medical Journal* in April 1919, who "set out to conquer [the influenza] disease have mightier opponents than Ludendorff or Hindenburg, and must face a longer campaign than that of 1914–1918."[13]

American novelist Katherine Anne Porter recounted the flu's impact in Denver, where she came down with the illness while working as a journalist during the war. In her semi-autobiographical short story about the flu epidemic, "Pale Horse, Pale Rider," Porter offered a realistic depiction of the effects of the disease from the point of view of one of its victims. Her protagonist, Miranda (whom she based on herself), contracts the flu, becoming delirious and hallucinating scenes that explicitly recalled the war. In a set of horrifying images, she believed she saw her physician killing a child. "Across the field came Dr. Hildesheim, his face a skull beneath his German helmet, carrying a naked infant writhing on the point of his bayonet, and a huge stone pot marked Poison in Gothic letters. He stopped before the well that Miranda remembered in a pasture on her father's farm, . . . and into its pure depths he threw the child and the poison, and the violated water sank back soundlessly into the earth. Miranda, screaming, ran with her arms over her head; her voice echoed and came back to her like a wolf's howl, Hildesheim is a Boche, a spy, a Hun, kill him, kill him before he kills you." In an episode of dissociation—a disruption of normal integration of conscious or physical functioning—Miranda described how "her mind, split in two, acknowledged and denied what she saw in the one instant, for across an abyss of complaining darkness her reasoning coherent self watched the strange frenzy of the other coldly, reluctant to admit the truth of its visions, its tenacious remorses and despairs."[14]

As Porter's story suggests, the flu left survivors with a variety of mental symptoms, many of them represented by physicians and the press in terms similar to those used after the war to describe sufferers of shell shock (Documents 12 and 13). Caroline Playne of Britain noted "the plague of nervous character" following the onslaught of influenza. Pronounced fatigue, lassitude, depression, sleeplessness, hallucinations, emotional lability, and even dissociation accompanied the physical debilitation of the disease. Dr. G. Holliday wrote to the *British Medical Journal* on August 17, 1918, that "mental symptoms were frequent" in the cases he saw; Samuel West informed readers of *The Lancet* on February 1, 1919, that "the depression which follows influenza is so constant that it ought to be regarded as part of the disease." The medical correspondent for *The Times* of London, having contracted the illness himself, advised readers that "the most distressing symptom was a swift loss of mental capacity and then inability to think coherently." "All forms of hysteria have been observed after influenza," reported Drs. Thomson and Thomson in 1919, "such as hysterical convulsions and the so-called hystero-epileptic attacks. . . . Post-influenzal neurasthenia is very familiar," they noted, "post-influenzal psychoses . . . frequently observed and reported." They cited a study that asserted that influenza, "of all the infectious diseases . . . is the most likely to be followed by mental disorder." *The Lancet* declared in December 1918 that "the 'higher centres' [of the nervous system] suffer chiefly. Marked depression is common, emotional instability is often seen, and suicide is by no means rare."[15]

Such psychological symptoms were vividly described by British writer Ivy Compton-Burnett, who came down with the flu in the summer of 1918 and was discovered by mere chance lying unconscious on the floor of her flat. She exhibited delirium and, when recovered from the acute stage of the disease, "extreme debility, unable to read or write." She asked to be read to, but could not tolerate much stimulus, asking her sister to "read, but don't put any expression into it. Read in a dull, monotonous voice." She took up mindless tasks as her recovery progressed, but "I couldn't do brainwork," she explained.[16]

A DEADLY FORCE GOES GLOBAL

The flu wreaked its havoc on military and civilian populations throughout the world in three waves. Arising first, we think, in the American Midwest in the late winter and early spring of 1918, it appears to have spread from Camp Funston outside Fort Riley, Kansas, to Camp Oglethorpe in Georgia, thence rapidly to Europe on board the troopships transporting U.S. forces to the western front (Documents 14–19). Contemporaries called it the "Spanish flu," mistakenly believing that it had originated in Spain. It had not, but Spain was one of the few countries in Europe that had not imposed an embargo on information emanating from its borders and allowed news reports of illness there to disseminate. Other European countries, engaged in a bloody, brutal, horrific war of attrition, censored what news could be put out and were quick to jump on Spain as the source of what would prove to be a terrible killer. An exhausted, emotionally and physically stressed European population proved no match for the illness, which marched through the continent, made its way to Asia and Africa, and arrived in Australasia in July 1918. (See Map 1.)

This first wave caused little alarm, as it was a fairly mild strain and killed no more than the usual number of influenza victims, but it was followed by an onslaught of unprecedented force. By mid-August the virus had mutated, and the second wave began to make itself felt, moving speedily along commercial and military transportation routes across the globe, leaving few populations untouched.

The new form of the virus landed in Freetown, Sierra Leone, in West Africa on August 15, carried by two hundred sick sailors who had traveled from Britain on board the British naval ship HMS *Mantua*. Within two weeks, local dockworkers had spread the flu into town, where perhaps as much as 3 percent of Sierra Leone's population died from the disease. They also carried the flu on board other ships tied up at Freetown, thus transporting the virus to other ports along the African coast. The *Shango* carried the disease from Freetown to Accra, Gold Coast (present-day Ghana), and on to the Cape Coast; the SS *Bida* took it from Sierra Leone to Lagos, Nigeria, in mid-September, from which it then spread inland along the railway lines, bicycle and walking paths, and streams carrying canoes upriver (Documents 20–24). Troopships *Jaroslav* and *Veronej*, calling at Freetown, transported 1,300 troops from the South African Native Labour Contingent, who had seen service in France, to Cape Town. As these men made their way home, they brought the virus into southern and central Africa.[17] (See Map 2.)

The second wave of the flu appeared in Brest, on the northwest coast of France, around August 22. Brest served as the disembarkation port for the American Expeditionary Force, some 1.6 million strong by September 1918. Some days later, influenza appeared in the United States, in Boston, the port from which a large portion of the American forces embarked en route to France. As arriving troops moved into their camps and then made their way to the western front, the virus moved with them, inflicting a heavy toll in illness and deaths among the fighting forces and the hard-pressed civilian populations of Europe.

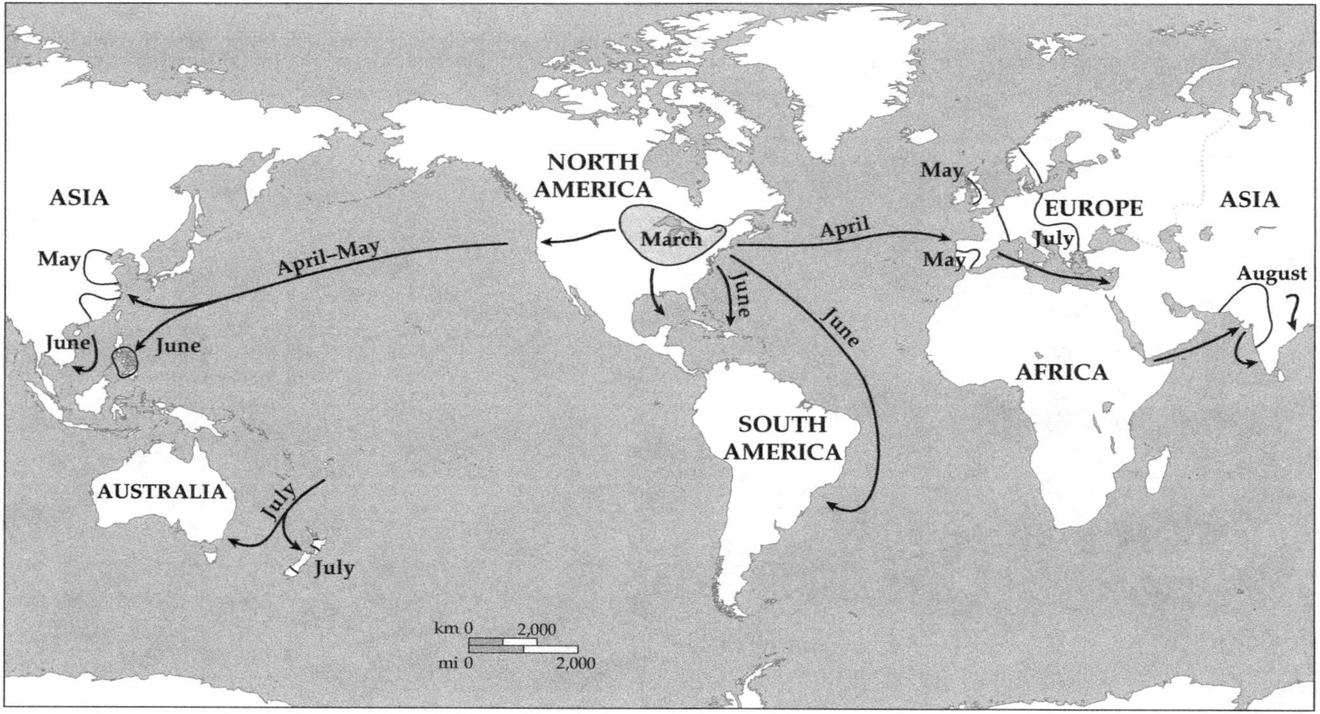

Map 1. *The First Wave, Spring 1918*

Influenza first appeared in the American Midwest in March of 1918. By April, it had made its way to Europe, Asia, and North Africa. By July 1918, it had appeared on six continents, hitting South America and the Pacific Islands in June, and Australia the following month. This first wave was relatively mild and caused little alarm.

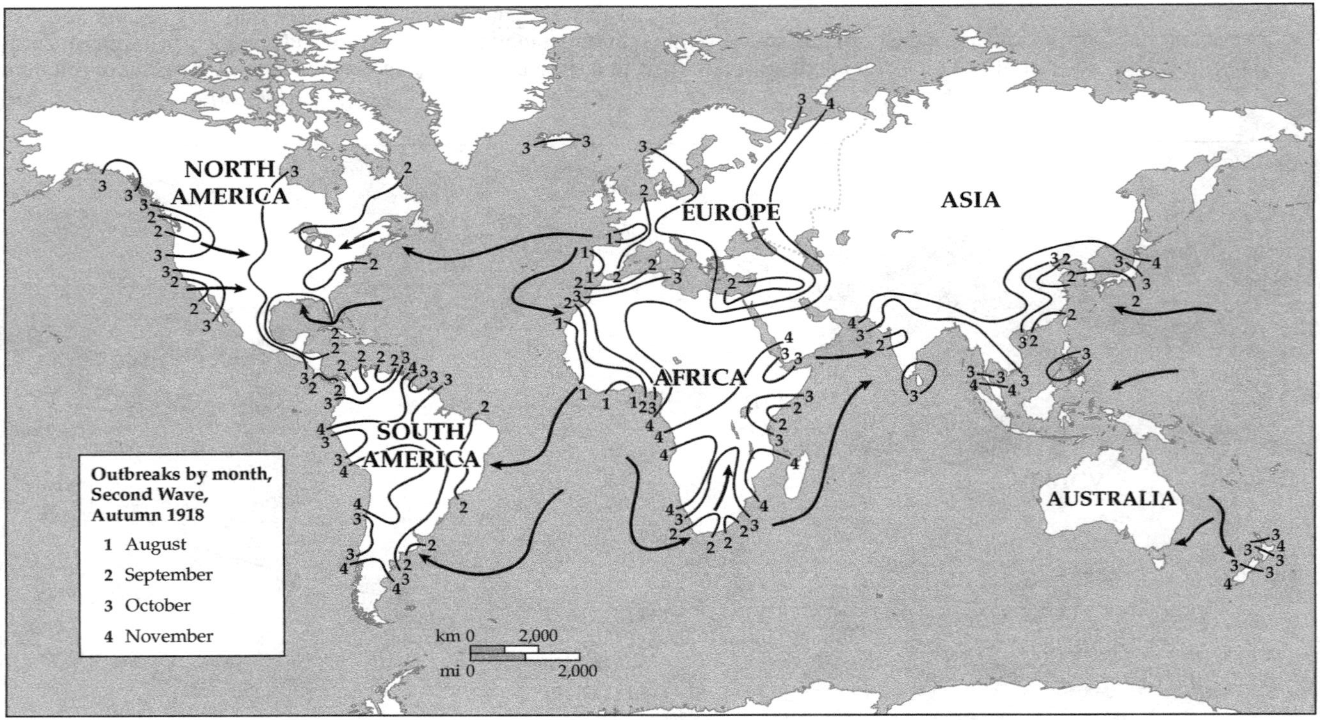

Map 2. *The Second Wave, Autumn 1918*
By August 1918, the virus had mutated into a deadlier and more virulent form. Carried on board commercial and military ships, it spread quickly through port towns and cities and into inland regions.

From Russia, the flu moved into Asia; it entered India through the port of Bombay in October. It made its way to Australia, New Zealand, and the Pacific Islands by November and December. From Boston, the flu traveled westward across the American continent and was also carried aboard ship to the Caribbean and to Central and South America. No part of the inhabited world escaped unscathed.[18]

The third wave of influenza appeared in February 1919; less virulent than the second, it nevertheless took its toll on already devastated populations.

The mortality figures for the flu pandemic beggar the imagination. Where influenza epidemics in the past produced death rates of about 0.1 percent of those infected, this one killed 2.5 percent of those infected. Britain lost 250,000 people to the disease, as did France and Germany. In the Russian empire, 450,000 inhabitants died, as disease combined with revolution and civil war to decimate the population; 50,000 died in Canada. In the United States, 675,000 Americans died, and life expectancy dropped by some twelve years in 1918 as a consequence of the huge numbers of deaths recorded that year. Indigenous peoples in North and Latin America and in Australia and New Zealand suffered disproportionate mortality rates; some communities lost upwards of 80 percent of their members.

Africans died in greater numbers than did Europeans: Where the latter experienced mortality rates of perhaps 1–2 percent, African rates reached upwards of 5 percent of the population. In Kenya, for example, 50,000 people, or 5.5 percent of the population, succumbed to the disease. South Africa lost perhaps 280,000. South Asia was hit hardest of all overall, India alone suffering the loss of at least six million and perhaps as many as fifteen million people (Document 25). Indonesian deaths reached 1.5 million. Within some populations, there was a great disparity in mortality groups; white New Zealanders, for example, had a death rate of 5.8 per 1,000, while the indigenous Maori population died at a rate about seven times higher.

China and Japan appear to have weathered the illness better than most other countries. Japan's death rate stood at 4.5 per thousand, while Shanghai's may have been as low as 1.3 per thousand. It is virtually impossible to know the death rate across China as a whole, as records simply do not exist that might reveal it, but what documents we do have suggest a far lower incidence of death than occurred in other parts of the world (Document 26).[19]

CHEASTY

TREATMENT RESPONSES: "THERE WAS JUST NOTHING YOU COULD DO"

Governments and public health officials responded to the epidemic in haphazard ways. At one extreme, German authorities simply refused to make public the extent to which the disease threatened the public health. In late May 1918, mention of the disease had entered Germany via foreign press agencies, which mistakenly attributed the origins of the outbreak of influenza to Spain, but a January 1918 directive had prohibited publication or public discussion of any statistics treating infections. Even when the more virulent strain of flu arrived in September, German state ministries and local bureaus denied or downplayed the incidence of illness and death.[20] In other countries where wartime restrictions on the dissemination of information were not so strict, authorities took pains to try to reduce the transmission of the disease. Schools, theaters, libraries, and other sites where crowds might congregate were shut down; bars and churches, however, were not. The public and their servants—police, nurses, bus drivers, soldiers and the like—were urged to wear surgical masks (Documents 28, 32, and 35). Advertisements touted the benefits of alcohol, tobacco, patent medicines, or home remedies containing garlic, camphor, cinnamon, quinine, or sugar cubes soaked in kerosene (Documents 36, 37, and 38).[21] Such remedies didn't work.

To their surprise, dismay, and chagrin, physicians did not know how to treat this disease. The documents in this volume reveal just how little Western scientists knew, misunderstanding the etiology of the illness and prescribing often-contradictory measures to treat it. Having mistaken its source as a bacillus, which since the 1890s had been thought to be the cause of influenza, doctors resorted to treatments that could have no effect on viruses, whose role in generating influenza was not discovered until 1933. Many physicians turned to vaccines to treat their patients, but these were bound to fail in the absence of any real knowledge about the disease's cause (Documents 29 and 42). Despite their efforts to treat the flu with almost any remedy they could think of

---

Opposite: The American Expeditionary Force Marching through Downtown Seattle, 1918

The civilian population had been ordered by authorities to wear masks in order to hinder transmission of the disease, a precaution that the military found necessary as well.

(Documents 42 and 43), ultimately they were helpless in the face of this disease. As one American physician put it, "There was just nothing you could do."[22] Western physicians in China excoriated and mocked traditional Chinese medicine (Document 44), little realizing that the treatments advised there included compounds—such as the untranslatable *mahuang xingren shigao decoction*, for example—that had been shown to reduce fever. Noting the effectiveness of Chinese traditional medicine in treating epidemic disease over a number of centuries, two Chinese scientists believe that the far lower rates of mortality in China were a result of peasants turning to traditional practitioners, whose successes in reducing fever by means of herbal remedies were long-standing.[23] In Japan, similarly, traditional treatments utilizing an oleo of dried ephedrine, peony, and gingerroot proved effective in reducing fever and nasal congestion. This herbal concoction was cheap and readily available to all but the poorest Japanese, and it may have helped to control the high fever that accompanied pneumonia.[24]

With physicians unable to make much difference during the pandemic, nursing care turned out to be one of the most effective treatments. Countries involved in fighting the Great War experienced a pronounced nursing shortage, however, so nurses were often in short supply. They died, moreover, in fairly large numbers, given their exposure to the disease (Document 47). Despite these factors, nurses brought relief to a great many patients, and their ability to make a difference to their patients served as a pointed contrast to the lack of effective treatment that physicians could produce. Physicians often reported their despair at making a difference; nurses, however, took pride in their ability to alleviate the suffering of many of their patients (Documents 45 and 46).

SHORT- AND LONG-TERM CONSEQUENCES OF THE PANDEMIC

The flu had a powerful impact on the early twentieth century, not only on the families, communities, societies, and nations that suffered such tremendous losses, but also on the politics and economics that characterized the interwar period. Individuals carried the burden of personal grief and tragedy throughout the course of their lives (Document 49). Economies suffered from the loss of workers and consumers; insurance companies faced liabilities greater than those incurred through wartime deaths (Document 27). Governments throughout the world were convinced by the experience of the flu to develop and institute public health systems. In South Africa, the Public Health Act of 1919, by removing poor white populations from slums and limiting its measures to white populations in urban centers, facilitated the racial segregation of cities. The Act did not utilize specifically racial language in its clauses, because legislators never considered that its provisions would include African populations. Thus, the racial segregation that Public Health Act helped to create lay the groundwork for the system of apartheid that emerged in South Africa after 1948[25] (Document 55). Elsewhere, material and emotional stresses contributed to anticolonial revolts that broke out in the decade following the war (Documents 57–59).

Although the flu epidemic appeared during the course of World War I and spread with the virulence it did via the presence of armies massed in Europe, little attention has been given to the impact the epidemic might have had on the prosecution and outcome of the war. The flu had a decided effect on the American Expeditionary Force as it engaged in its massive campaign against the Central Powers in the Meuse-Argonne battle in late September, October, and early November 1918. Of the four million men of the AEF, at least one million fell ill with flu, compelling General John Pershing, commander of the AEF, to make increasingly urgent appeals to Washington for increased medical support. "Influenza exists in epidemic form among our troops in many localities in France accompanied by many serious cases of pneumonia," he cabled on October 3, a week into the Meuse-Argonne campaign. "Request 1500 members of Army Nurse Corps . . . be sent to France as an emergency requirement."[26] The Eighty-Eighth Division, serving on the front lines, reported that about 30 percent of its forces had come down with the flu; of these men, 45 percent died during one week in October. The Eighty-Sixth Division saw a 35 percent rate of illness among its ranks, and some companies in the division had rates of up to 73 percent. This meant that replacement troops for those killed or wounded at the front could not be readily found, and the ability to evacuate and treat the wounded was bogged down by the numbers of soldiers and medical personnel ill with influenza. Though the Americans defeated the Germans in the Meuse-Argonne sector, Pershing's efforts were considerably hampered by the incidence of disease. More Americans died of disease than of the infliction of bullets or shells, and many thousands of men died who might otherwise have lived had they been able to reach military hospitals equipped to handle their injuries.[27]

The flu may also have had an impact on the German effort to end the war through a last massive offensive in the west in the spring of 1918. The treaty of Brest-Litovsk with Russia in 1918 had freed up German troops in the east, enabling their transport to the western front for use in what the German high command hoped would be a knockout blow against the British and French armies. With an additional one million experienced soldiers and three thousand guns, German forces outnumbered those of the Allies considerably, by as many as four to one in some sectors along the western front. British forces had been seriously weakened during the Battle for Passchendaele in 1917, and the French army had suffered not only heavy losses but was faced with internal disagreement at the highest levels of command. General Pershing had refused to commit American troops to the British and French armies. German generals Paul von Hindenburg and Erich von Ludendorff, directing not merely the war effort but virtually the whole government as well, realized that they had one last chance to break through Allied lines. Their hopes for victory rested upon this final assault.

On March 21, the Germans launched what has come to be called the Spring Offensive. They broke through British lines near Saint-Quentin; by the end of May, the Germans advanced on the Marne River, establishing artillery guns that could fire on Paris, which led the French government to prepare to evacuate from the capital. But when Ludendorff ordered a final push on July 15, 1918, his offensive failed, allowing the Allies to counterattack, which they did, beginning August 8 at the Second Battle of the Marne. Joined now by the Americans, the Allies pushed back the German forces, until Hindenburg and Ludendorff were forced to sue for peace. The armistice that ended the war in favor of the Allies went into effect on November 11, 1918.

The failure of the German armies to complete their offensive in May spelled their defeat. German troops lacked sufficient food and supplies and they were sick, Ludendorff reporting that more than two thousand soldiers in each of his divisions suffered from influenza (Documents 50, 52, and 53).[28] Most scholars have dismissed the flu as a major factor in this defeat, arguing that because the flu simultaneously hit all of the belligerent countries with comparable effect, it had little to do with the German defeat.[29] But one recent scholar has asserted that in fact German and Austrian forces experienced a particularly virulent form of the virus during the Spring Offensive, some two months *before* the disease struck the Allied forces so heavily in August, September, and October (Document 51). Between the time the offensive began in March until its failure in mid-July, 1.75 million German soldiers had become ill with the flu, more than 500,000 of them in June and July. Ludendorff, by late July, was attributing his failure to continue the German offensive against the Allies in part to the effects of the pandemic (Document 50).[30] Historians share the belief that had the German Spring Offensive succeeded, Britain and France would have been compelled to accede to German demands for a peace settlement. Its failure, in light of the debilitating conditions faced by the armed forces and the civilian population at home, virtually ensured an Allied victory once the Americans appeared on the scene. Some German units experienced infection rates of 80 percent, while on the home front, civilian mortality rates reached their highest level for the entire wartime period in October and November of 1918. The German workforce had become weakened considerably by flu between March and November 1918, and their productivity waned concomitantly, as measured by the records of coal mine output.[31] It cannot be asserted that influenza brought about the defeat of Germany in 1918; too many other factors played important roles in the failure of the Germans to defeat their enemies. However, the incapacity of the German soldiers who had fallen ill during the flu epidemic and the inability of the German home front to supply and feed its troops contributed to the failure of the Spring Offensive.

Elsewhere, the devastations caused by influenza contributed to a variety of postwar colonial revolts. In India, which had already been hit so heavily by famine and disease, the influenza epidemic struck the Punjab province particularly hard, killing up to 25 percent of the population in some villages (Document 25).[32] Further, conditions in the Punjab following the war made life difficult for a broad strata of the Indian population. Wages in industries that had prospered in wartime fell dramatically, catapulting much of the population into debt. Weakened and impoverished Punjabis often expressed their distress through protests, creating disorder throughout the province; Mohandas Gandhi and his Congress Party made a clear connection between the extent of famine, influenza, and riots throughout India in *Young India*, the official organ of the Congress Party (Document 60). Colonial officials sought and received exceptional new powers to deal with the disorders by means of the Rowlatt Acts, legislation that enabled the British viceroy to suspend due process of law and to imprison Indians without trial. The Rowlatt Acts inflamed Indian public opinion, and educated Indians of all political stripes submerged their differences and united against the Rowlatt Acts under Gandhi's *satyagraha* (civil disobedience) movement. Demonstrations took place in a number of cities, and rioting broke out in Ahmadabad, Delhi, and a number of Punjab provinces (Document 61). When, on March 30 and April 6, 1919, a series of peaceful *hartals*—a kind of religious general strike—shut down much of the Punjab, rumors of mutinies and plots to end British rule swept through the Anglo-Indian population. Believing themselves to be at risk for assault and murder, British officials and civilians began to arm themselves.[33]

In Amritsar, British officials ordered the arrest and deportation of two local leaders, who, they believed, planned to incite the townspeople to violence. Word of their deportation spread throughout the city, and, in concert with news of Gandhi's arrest in Palwal the previous day, spurred large crowds of Indians—unarmed—to congregate in the city center and make their way to the Civil Lines, the boundary separating the Indian from the Anglo-Indian population, to protest the arrests. Along the way, no violence occurred and no Europeans were assaulted. Upon their arrival at the bridges that crossed over the Civil Lines, however, the crowd met resistance from British troops, one of whom may have fired a shot without orders; when demonstrators tried to continue forward and began throwing stones at the troops, they were fired upon. Official accounts put the Indian dead at twelve, the wounded at twenty to thirty. The shooting set off a day of rioting that resulted in sabotage, looting, arson, assault, and the deaths by beating of five European men. Protesters cut telegraph and telephone lines and damaged the railways. Anglo-Indian women and children were hurried off to the fort occupied by British forces, but not before an Englishwoman was badly beaten and left for dead in the street.[34]

On April 13, 1919, Brigadier-General Reginald Dyer ordered a patrol of Indian troops under his command to fire on a crowd of some 25,000 unarmed Indian men, women, and children in the Jallianwala Bagh, a kind of walled garden, in Amritsar. About ten minutes later, their ammunition virtually spent, he ordered the troops to cease shooting. Hundreds of people lay dead, thousands more wounded littered the ground. Dyer led his troops from the Bagh, leaving the injured to fend for themselves; the curfew imposed on Amritsar kept would-be rescuers from collecting the dead and getting medical attention for the wounded until the next day. Many died overnight. The Amritsar massacre, as it came to be called, provoked a crisis in British and Indian affairs. For Indian nationalists, it marked the moment at which home rule within the empire would no longer be enough; nothing less than independence would do and the "Quit India" movement took off.

In this instance, colonial revolt occurred immediately following the depredations of the influenza pandemic. In southeastern Nigeria, colonial resentments born of the pandemic would fester for a decade, slowly fostering what would eventually become a series of remarkable revolts.[35] In November and December of 1929, a series of demonstrations, protests, risings, and riots involving tens of thousands of women took place in southeast Nigeria. The Aba Riots, as the British dubbed them, are known to their participants and to subsequent African memory and historiography as the *Ogu Umunwaayi*, the Women's War. In the course of it, more than fifty southeastern Nigeria women were killed by British troops.[36] The Women's War marked a historical high point in the West African resistance to British colonialism, as southeastern Nigerian women sought to defend their social systems, which had been dramatically transformed by their engagement with British colonialism. A growing imbalance in socioeconomic relations between southeastern Nigerian men and women; the displacement of indigenous religious and economic practices by Christianity and European capitalism; the undermining of indigenous power structures by the British colonial administration—all these had affected southeastern Nigerian peoples since the late nineteenth century. The twin traumas of the Great War and influenza brought even more profound and extended upheaval, with the flu constituting perhaps the greatest disruption of all. The Women's War represented an attempt on the part of women to, in effect, decolonize southeastern Nigeria, to return their societies to the practices of the past.

Nigerians attributed the flu epidemic to the British, calling it "the white man's death. They shoot it into the air, and we breathe it in and die."[37] This was a disease unlike others such as smallpox, to which Nigerians were accustomed. It felled men in their fields with virtually no warning. "Death was always so sudden that the relatives were too shocked to cry," noted author Buchi Emecheta, who recounted her mother's experiences during the flu in her novel, *The Slave Girl* (Document 59). Families and villages suffered its ravages, sometimes whole villages succumbing to death; the mortality wrought by the epidemic had the effect of undermining long-held family and community responsibilities and contributed to social disintegration, the effects of which fell disproportionately on women. Officials estimated that 250,000 people out of a population of nine million in the southern provinces of Nigeria died from the flu, although these are wildly undercounted figures. While colonial officials reported that "women suffered less than men" in the pandemic, they also noted that there was greater incidence of illness among pregnant women than in the female population more generally.[38]

This demographic fact resonates with women's contentions later in the *Ogu* that pregnant women were perceived as the particular targets of all that had gone wrong in the land—that the "trees that bear fruit" were seen as particularly vulnerable to the social transformations and traumas associated with British rule, including the new killer, *ifelunza* or *felenza*, as Igbo-speaking people called it.

Women bore the brunt of extra work imposed by the pandemic. In the generality of southeastern Nigerian households, women cared for the sick and the dying almost exclusively. When men died, married women were expected to prepare their corpses for burial and to undergo at least some of the privations of widowhood[39] on top of their own illness and grief. If men survived and convalesced, married women would be expected to take care of them as well as any children that might have survived, while also maintaining their household duties. Women were also expected, during this *oge ifelunza* (time period of the influenza), to take on the responsibilities of cultivation when men could not work. Emecheta places the flu epidemic at the center of *The Slave Girl*, a story that culminates in a women's war. The narrative thread carries the action of the novel from the devastation of family and community by the disease, to slavery, to women's war, to freedom from slavery, to a return to home and family—opening and closing with *felenza*. Emecheta learned about the epidemic at her mother's knee, and while we cannot claim the novel for historical "fact" (the flu is said to have broken out in 1916, for example), we must see in it traces of the powerful influence exerted by the influenza epidemic on southeastern Nigerian peoples; it contributed to the single most powerful memory of rebellion against colonial authority, the Women's War of 1929.

Perhaps most intriguing, the influenza epidemic may have had some role to play in the peace settlement imposed on Germany following the Great War. The major politicians charged with creating the Versailles Treaty—President Woodrow Wilson of the United States, Prime Minister David Lloyd George of Great Britain, and Prime Minister Georges Clemenceau of France—all fell victim to the flu.[40] The physical and mental debilitation that Wilson suffered, in particular, may have had an impact on the kind of peace enshrined in the treaty, whose punitive nature contributed to the acceptance of fascism in Germany. In January 1918, Wilson had issued his Fourteen Points, principles according to which a non-punitive peace between the belligerent countries should be forged; it was on the basis of the Fourteen Points that Germany had signed the armistice in November 1918. Clemenceau and Lloyd

George had different ideas about peace terms, looking to impose on their defeated enemy measures that would (1) require Germany to pay reparations (that is, pay the Allies for the costs they had incurred in prosecuting the war); and (2) permit the Allies to occupy the Rhineland and the Saar Basin, resource-rich areas of Germany. Wilson was determined to defeat such punitive measures and to ensure the creation of a just peace.

When delegates to the peace conference arrived in Paris in the spring of 1919, the third wave of the flu had just peaked. Many of the chief actors and their behind-the-scenes aides fell ill with the disease. Disease continued into April and struck Wilson at a particularly difficult moment in negotiations. He and Clemenceau had parted ways over the issues of reparations and French annexation of the Saar Basin, and on April 3, it appeared that Wilson might walk out of the talks. That night, Wilson suddenly came down with the flu, producing a temperature of 103°F, a cough so extreme that he could hardly breathe, and debilitating diarrheal cramps. His physician, Admiral Cary Grayson, feared he might die that night. He didn't, but over the next five days, Wilson lay prostrate, unable to get out of bed (Document 62).

Ten days after Wilson fell ill, the difficulties standing in the way of an Anglo-American-French agreement on reparations, occupation of the Rhineland, and annexation of the Saar Basin were resolved. While a great many concessions had been granted, Wilson lost by far the greatest number. Virtually none of his Fourteen Points save the establishment of a League of Nations survived, and the treaty that was forced upon the Germans contained a number of harsh terms. The loss of the Rhineland and the Saar meant that Germany's economic recovery would be considerably hampered. Article 231, the so-called war guilt clause, compelled Germany to accept "the responsibility of Germany and her allies for causing all the loss and damage to which the Allied and Associated Governments and their nationals have been subjected as a consequence of the war imposed upon them by the aggression of Germany and her allies," legitimating the imposition of heavy reparations payments. Germany was forced to demilitarize and to cede significant amounts of territory containing German populations. German colonies were ostensibly placed under the mandate of the League, but were effectively handed over to Britain and France. Wilson's "peace without victory" lay in tatters.[41]

How did this happen? Some individuals close to Wilson attributed his failure to insist upon his principles to the effects of the flu. Not only did the disease weaken him physically, it seemed also to have produced the same mental symptoms of depression, disorientation, and delusion described earlier (Documents 63 and 64). "I never knew the President to be in such a difficult frame of mind as he is now," wrote his secretary, Gilbert Close, on April 7, 1919. "Even while lying in bed he manifested peculiarities." Wilson's Secret Service agent observed that "he never did regain his physical strength, and his weakness of body naturally reacted upon his mind. He lacked his old quickness of grasp." Lacking the energy, the intellectual capacity, and even the interest to continue his battle with Lloyd George and Clemenceau, he simply gave in and assented to a peace so unjust that, he told an aide in early May, "if I were a German, I think I should not sign it."[42] Faced with the prospect of a continuing Allied blockade that had reduced the German civilian population to starvation, German officials had no choice but to sign. The humiliations and material deprivations forced upon the German people by the Versailles Treaty, among other factors, gave ammunition to antidemocratic forces in Germany that would ultimately allow for the rise of Nazism and the ascent to power of Adolf Hitler in 1933.

This is not to suggest that the influenza epidemic of 1918–1919 brought about the rise of fascism and the outbreak of the Second World War in Europe. That would be far too direct a connection and cannot be sustained by the evidence. But the epidemic may well have had a significant effect on the outcome of the peace settlement following World War I, and its potential role should not go unremarked.

LEGACY AND LESSONS OF THE PANDEMIC

In 1933, scientists determined that influenza was caused by a virus, not by a bacillus as they had previously believed. Isolation of the virus enabled clinicians to develop vaccines against the disease, but because virus strains contain so many subtypes and because they mutate so rapidly in a process known as antigenic drift, vaccines are not always effective from year to year—even in the unlikely event that they could be made available to large segments of the world's population. Flu pandemics broke out again in 1957 and 1968, but none of them struck with anything like the virulence seen in 1918.

Incredibly, the influenza epidemic of 1918–1919 disappeared from popular memory for more than six decades following its spectacular visitation upon the peoples of the world. As we've seen, individuals wrote of it in their memoirs or biographies, but public consciousness of the extraordinary losses and the traumas they brought about simply vanished. In the 1970s, two textbooks addressing the pandemic appeared,[43] but the significance of the disease in the history of most nations simply did not register.

We can only speculate as to why this historical amnesia settled in and lasted so long. A number of explanations suggest themselves. First, the devastations and dislocations of the Great War proved so profound in their consequences that influenza just didn't signify. The Russian Revolution, the dismantling of world empires, the Great Depression, the rise of fascism, World War II, the cold war, and decolonization—these momentous events arose out of World War I and commanded the attention and the energies of the world for much of the twentieth century. But perhaps equally important, the experiences of the flu pandemic of 1918–1919 laid bare the inability of nations and peoples to prevent, control, or treat what had come to be regarded as an everyday illness. Science had failed; medicine had failed; governments had failed—and what were people supposed to do with that nasty bit of information? Forgetting about it may just have appealed to publics too frightened to acknowledge so grand a failure on the part of institutions and agencies they had come to rely upon for protection and safety.

Whatever might have caused us to relegate the pandemic to our historical unconscious, we appear to have dredged it up again in the 1990s, no doubt in response in part to the AIDS epidemic that had engulfed the world in the 1980s. Scholarly accounts of 1918 appeared in greater profusion, and new interest, along with vastly improved technology, enabled scientists to revisit the events of 1918 with far more effective tools of investigation. In 1997 scientists under the leadership of Jeffrey Taubenberger determined the virus that had been responsible for the terrible pandemic of 1918–1919. Using preserved lung tissue samples from the body of U.S. Army Private Roscoe Vaughan, who had died of the flu at Camp Jackson, South Carolina, on September 26, 1918, Taubenberger and his colleagues performed DNA analyses. The tests revealed that the flu pandemic of 1918–1919 had been caused by an influenza A virus, H1N1.

The pandemics of 1957 and 1968 were caused by different variants of the H2N2 virus, which had completely displaced H1N1 in an unprecedentedly rapid manner. Survivors of the 1918 disease enjoyed immunity from H1N1 but not from H2N2, and they and those born after 1919 came down with the flu in large numbers. Fortunately, mortality rates remained relatively low. In 2009, H1N1 appeared in populations across the globe, spawning fears that another pandemic like that of 1918–1919 might recur. In June 2009 the World Health Organization (WHO) announced that a pandemic had indeed broken out, and public health authorities around the world mobilized quickly to provide information designed both to caution and to reassure people about the nature of the illness.[44] "Wash your hands," we were advised over and over again; "stay home if you've contracted the flu"; "get the H1N1 flu shot." Vaccines to prevent the illness were rushed into production, although they did not appear in time to meet the demand for them in many parts of the United States.

As it turned out, this strain of H1N1 didn't hit with the same force as it had in 1918 and 1919, although the same pattern of illness among people aged fifteen to forty-five emerged, and many people worldwide died from the virus. "At the time, the stories were coming out—we didn't know a lot about this new virus and it was hard to know how alarmed we should be," noted Dr. Connie Price of Denver Health Medical Center in Denver, Colorado. "I think looking back, we gave it a lot of attention and it wasn't as severe as we initially anticipated, but we didn't know that at the time."[45] The virus simply did not possess the virulence to attack with the same intensity it enjoyed in 1918, but the lessons learned from that unprecedented pandemic informed the decision making of public health authorities to get the word out about taking this illness seriously. Educational efforts and immediate action on the part of public health authorities are crucial elements of any response to a suspected outbreak of pandemic disease, but governments also face the problem of "crying wolf" when potential outbreaks don't pan out, causing populations to tune out the messages they need to hear in order to protect themselves from illness and even death. The world seems to have dodged a bullet in 2009, but virologists expect that another influenza pandemic will emerge and sometimes worry that it will possess the capacity of its 1918 forerunner to outrun our ability to manage it.[46]

NOTES

[1] Thirty million is a conservative estimate. Those estimates that go as high as one hundred million are difficult to document, but reflect extrapolations of data that have been recorded. Record keeping, in the midst of such an enormous event, can be expected to be haphazard at best, especially among medical officials fighting to keep patients alive. And many medical officials differentiated deaths from influenza from those due to pneumonia, which proved to be the real killer in the pandemic.

[2] Ministry of Health, *Report on the Pandemic of Influenza, 1918–19* (London: His Majesty's Stationery Office, 1920–1921), iv, xiv, 69.

[3] Howard Phillips and David Killingray, eds., *The Spanish Influenza Pandemic of 1918–19: New Perspectives* (London: Routledge, 2003), 4–5; Niall Johnson, *Britain and the 1918–19 Influenza Pandemic: A Dark Epilogue* (London: Routledge, 2006), 162.

[4] Dr. Ijiro Gomibuchi, *Personal Account of the World Influenza Epidemic of 1918–1919, with Remarks on the Use of Diphtheria Serum* (May 1919), trans. Edwina Palmer and Geoffrey Rice, "A Japanese Physician's Response to Pandemic Influenza: Ijiro Gombuchi and the 'Spanish Flu' in Yaita-Cho, 1918–1919," *Bulletin of the History of Medicine* 66 (1992): 569.

[5] Letter from William Collier, *The Lancet*, October 26, 1918, 567; Ministry of Health, *Report on the Pandemic*, 72; Phillips and Killingray, *The Spanish Influenza Pandemic*, 5.

[6] Letter from William Collier, *The Lancet*, October 26, 1918, 567; Ministry of Health, *Report on the Pandemic*, p. 72.

[7] Jeffrey Taubenberger, "Genetic Characterisation of the 1918 'Spanish' Influenza Virus," in Phillips and Killingray, *The Spanish Influenza Pandemic*, 40, 41.

[8] Douglas Almond, "Is the 1918 Influenza Pandemic Over? Long-Term Effects of *In Utero* Influenza Exposure in the Post-1940 U.S. Population," *Journal of Political Economy* 114, no. 4 (August 2006): 681.

[9] Andrew Price-Smith, *Contagion and Chaos: Disease, Ecology, and National Security in the Era of Globalization* (Cambridge, Mass.: MIT Press, 2009), 60–61.

[10] Ministry of Health, *Report on the Pandemic*, 67; "The Prevention of Influenza," *The Lancet*, March 1, 1919, 347.

[11] Thomas A. Garrett, "Economic Effects of the 1918 Influenza Pandemic. Implications for a Modern-day Pandemic," Federal Reserve Bank of St. Louis (November 2007): 19, 20. www.stlouisfed.org/community/development/assets/pdf/pandemic-flu-report.pdf.

[12] Carol R. Byerly, *Fever of War: The Influenza Epidemic in the U.S. Army during World War* I (New York: New York University Press, 2005), 93–94.

[13] "Growing Toll of Influenza," *Daily Express*, July 3, 1918, 3; Charles Graves, *Invasion By Virus. Can It Happen Again*? (London: Icon Books, 1969), p. 32; *Illustrated London News*, July 20, 1918, 83; *Daily Express*, October 31, 1918, 3; *Daily Express*, October 15, 1918, 3; David Thomson and Robert Thomson, *Influenza. Annals of the Pickett-Thomson Research Laboratory*, Monograph XVI, Part I (London: Baillière, Tindall & Cox, 1933), 738; *British Medical Journal*, April 5, 1919, 418.

[14] Katherine Anne Porter, "Pale Horse, Pale Rider," *The Collected Stories of Katherine Anne Porter* (New York: Harcourt Brace, 1965), 309.

[15] Caroline E. Playne, *Britain Holds On, 1917, 1918* (London: George Allen & Unwin, 1933), 389; *British Medical Journal*, August 17, 1918, 159; *The Lancet*, February 1, 1919, 196; qtd. in Graves, *Invasion by Virus*, 25–26; Thomson and Thomson, *Influenza*, 789, 796; Sir Thomas Horder, MD, "Some Observations on the More Severe Cases of Influenza Occurring during the Present Epidemic," *The Lancet*, December 28, 1918, 872.

[16] Hilary Spurling, *Ivy, The Life of I. Compton-Burnett* (New York: Knopf, 1984), 238, 239.

[17] Phillips and Killingray, "Introduction," *The Spanish Influenza*, 6, 7, 9.

[18] Ibid., 6–7, 8, 10.

[19] Phillips and Killingray, "Introduction," *The Spanish Influenza Pandemic*, 7–10; Geoffrey W. Rice, "Japan and New Zealand in the 1918 Influenza Pandemic: Comparative

Perspectives on Official Responses and Crisis Management," in Phillips and Killingray, *The Spanish Influenza Pandemic*, 83; K. F. Cheng and P. C. Leung, "What Happened in China during the 1918 Influenza Pandemic?" *International Journal of Infectious Diseases* 11, no. 4 (July 2007): 360–64.

[20] Wilfried Witte, "The Plague That Was Not Allowed to Happen: German Medicine and the Influenza Epidemic of 1918–19 in Baden," in Phillips and Killingray, *The Spanish Influenza Pandemic*, 49–51.

[21] Phillips and Killingray, "Introduction," *The Spanish Influenza Pandemic*, 8. See also Rice, "Japan and New Zealand in the 1918 Influenza Pandemic," in Phillips and Killingray, *The Spanish Influenza Pandemic*, 83; "Quinine and Cinnamon to the Rescue," *Daily Express*, June 22, 1918, 3.

[22] Qtd. in Nancy K. Bristow, "'You Can't Do Anything for Influenza,' Doctors, Nurses and the Power of Gender during the Influenza Pandemic in the United States," in Phillips and Killingray, *The Spanish Influenza Pandemic*, 61.

[23] Cheng and Leung, "What Happened in China during the 1918 Influenza Pandemic?" 360–64.

[24] Taubenberger, "Genetic Characterisation of the 1918 'Spanish' Influenza Virus," in Phillips and Killingray, *The Spanish Influenza Pandemic*, 40, 41; and Rice, "Japan and New Zealand in the 1918 Influenza Pandemic" in Phillips and Killingray, *The Spanish Influenza Pandemic*, 83.

[25] Susan Parnell, "Creating Racial Privilege: The Origins of South African Public Health and Town Planning Legislation," *Journal of Southern African Studies* 19, no. 3 (September 1993): 472, 488.

[26] Byerly, *Fever of War*, 113; qtd. in Alfred W. Crosby, *America's Forgotten Pandemic: The Influenza of 1918* (Cambridge, U.K.: Cambridge University Press, 1989), 157.

[27] Byerly, *Fever of War*, 112, 113, 116, 122.

[28] Michael B. A. Oldstone, *Viruses, Plagues, and History* (New York: Oxford University Press, 1998), 173.

[29] See, for example, Johnson, *Britain and the 1918–19 Influenza Pandemic*, 191.

[30] Price-Smith, *Contagion and Chaos*, 68.

[31] Ibid., 72.

[32] Collett, *Butcher of Amritsar*, 223.

[33] Ibid., 227.

[34] Government of India, *Disorders Inquiry Report, 1919–1920, Volume II* (Calcutta: Superintendent Government Printing, 1920), 32, 33.

[35] Matthew Heaton argues that the experience of the flu had no significant impact on the subsequent history of Nigerian anticolonial activity, but his analysis ends in 1918 and doesn't examine long-term events. See Michael M. Heaton, "The Press, Politics and Historical Memory: The Influenza Pandemics of 1918 and 1957 in Lagos Newspapers," in Toyin Falola and Matthew M. Heaton, *Traditional and Modern Health Systems in Nigeria* (Trenton, N.J.: Africa World Press, 2006).

[36] See Marc Matera, Misty L. Bastian, and Susan Kingsley Kent, *The Women's War of 1929: Gender and Violence in Colonial Nigeria* (Basingstoke, U.K.: Palgrave Macmillan, 2011), chap. 3.

[37] Buchi Emecheta, *The Slave Girl* (New York: George Braziller, 1977), 25.

[38] Don C. Ohadike, "The Influenza Pandemic of 1918–19 and the Spread of Cassava Cultivation on the Lower Niger: A Study in Historical Linkages," *Journal of African History* 23, no. 3 (1981): 384.

[39] Joseph Theresa Agbasiere, *Women in Igbo Life and Thought* (London: Routledge, 2000), 143–62.

[40] John Barry, *The Great Influenza* (New York: Viking, 2004), 383.

[41] See Harold Nicolson, *Peacemaking 1919* (New York: Grosset & Dunlap, 1965), 41–42.

[42] Crosby, *America's Forgotten Pandemic*, 189–95.

[43] See Richard Collier, *The Plague of the Spanish Lady* (New York: Atheneum, 1974), and Crosby, *America's Forgotten Pandemic.*

[44] See the information offered by the Centers for Disease Control at www.cdc.gov/H1N1flu/qa.htm.

[45] "The H1N1 Pandemic That Hasn't Really Happened," 9News Web site (KUSA-TV Multimedia Holdings Corporation), March 3, 2010.

[46] John S. Oxford, "A Virologist's Foreword," in Phillips and Killingray, *The Spanish Influenza*, xix.

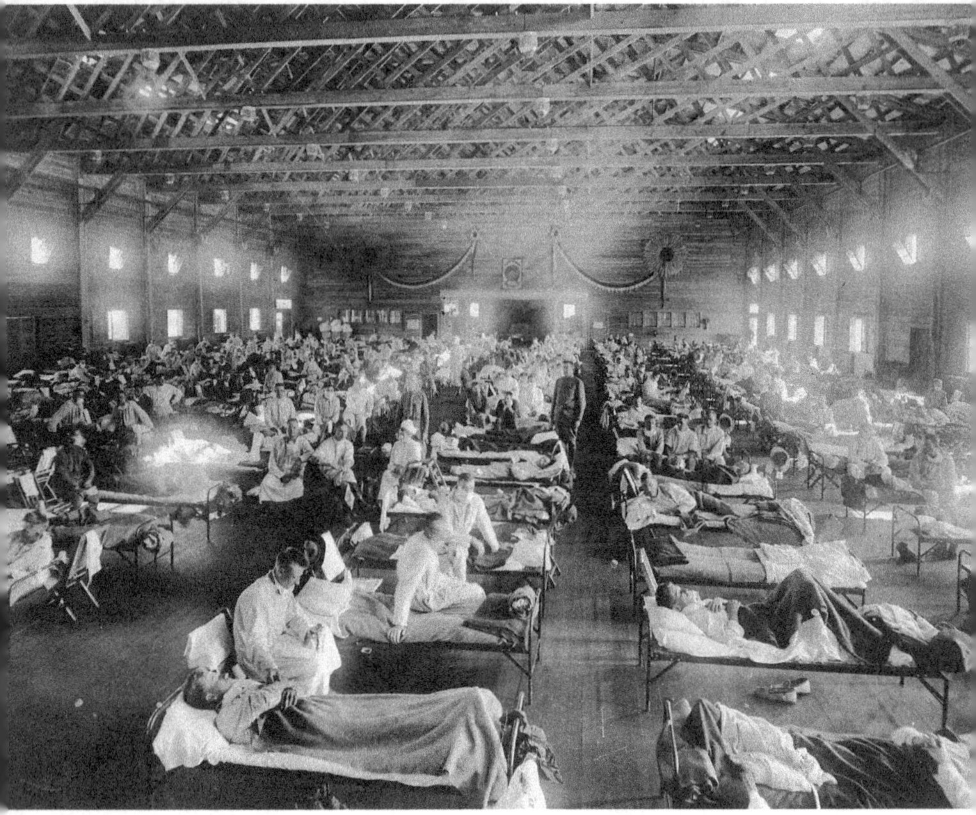

Soldiers Being Treated for Influenza at Camp Funston, Kansas, 1918
National Museum of Health and Medicine.

PART TWO

The Documents

1

The Nature and Experience of the Disease

1

Letter from a Volunteer Nurse

October 17, 1918

For those who cared for the victims, the influenza pandemic was an immensely personal experience. In this letter to a friend, a young Native American woman details her experiences in the autumn of 1918. Lutiant (last name unknown) attended the United States Indian Industrial Training School in Haskell, Kansas, a boarding school for Indian children that sought to eliminate their Indian ways and render them culturally and psychologically "American." She was working for the Department of the Interior in Washington, D.C., when the flu broke out and volunteered to work as a nurse at a nearby army camp. Her (inaccurate) assertion that two German spies had masqueraded as doctors to introduce the flu to the soldiers was a recurring motif, as shown in Documents 23 and 34.

Dear friend Louise:

So everybody has the "Flu" at Haskell? . . . As many as 90 people die every day here with the "Flu." Soldiers too, are dying by the dozens. So far, Felicity, C. Zane, and I are the only ones of the Indian girls who have not had it. We certainly consider ourselves lucky too, believe me. Katherine and I just returned last Sunday evening from Camp Humphrey "Somewhere in Virginia" where we volunteered to help nurse soldiers

Letter from nurse to her friend at the Haskell Indian Nations University, Kansas, October 17, 1918. Bureau of Indian Affairs. Record held at National Archives–Central Plains Region (Kansas City). Record Group 75.

sick with the Influenza. We were there at the Camp ten days among some of the very worse cases and yet we did not contract it. We had intended staying much longer than we did, but the work was entirely too hard for us, and anyway the soldiers were all getting better, so we came home to rest up a bit. We were day nurses and stationed in the Officer's barracks for six days and then transferred to the Private's barracks or hospital and were there four days before we came back. All nurses were required to work twelve hours a day—we worked from seven in the morning until seven at night, with only a short time for luncheon and dinner.

Believe me, we were always glad when night came because we sure did get tired. We had the actual Practical nursing to do—just like the other nurses had, and were given a certain number of wards with three or four patients in each of them to look after. Our chief duties were to give medicines to the patients, take temperatures, fix ice packs, feed them at "eating time," rub their back or chest with camphorated sweet oil, make egg-nogs, and a whole string of other things I can't begin to name. I liked the work just fine, but it was too hard, not being used to it. When I was in the Officer's barracks, four of the officers of whom I had charge, died. Two of them were married and called for their wife nearly all the time. It was sure pitiful to see them die. I was right in the wards alone with them each time, and Oh! The first one that died sure unnerved me—I had to go to the nurses' quarters and cry it out. The other three were not so bad. Really, Louise, Orderlies carried the dead soldiers out on stretchers at the rate of two every three hours for the first two days [we] were there. Two German spies, posing as doctors, were caught giving these Influenza germs to the soldiers and they were shot last Saturday at sunrise. It is such a horrible thing, it is hard to believe, and yet such things happen almost every day in Washington.

Repeated calls come from the Red Cross for nurses to do district work right here in D.C. I volunteered again, but as yet I have not been called and am waiting. Really, they are certainly "hard up" for nurses—*even me* can volunteer as a nurse in a camp or in Washington. . . .

2

E. T. HSIEH

The Recent Epidemic of Influenza in Peking

1918

Dr. E.T. Hsieh conducted research on patients suffering from influenza in the Laboratory at the Peking Union Medical College Hospital in what is today Beijing, China. His training and practice followed those of Western physicians; indeed, the journal in which his article is published issued English-language editions. Here, Hsieh describes the symptoms of the disease, as well as the manner in which it was then believed to be spread.

The recent epidemic appeared in Peking on October 6, 1918, and soon spread all over the city. It was prevalent also in Tientsin, Paotingfu, and many cities along the railroad lines. This proved to be a serious epidemic, with a high percentage of deaths. Half of our nurses and internes [*sic*] were infected. . . .

The onset of the disease is sudden. The initial chill is followed by a fever, reaching 102–103° F., or even 106.6° F. as I saw in one case in the Tehchow hospital. There is headache and general pain. . . .

After three or four days the crisis comes, when the patient is much relieved. Shortly after the fall, a relapse of the fever occurs in some cases. With the rise in temperature, the respiratory symptoms are much worse, likewise the sore throat. . . .

As the bacillus has very poor resistance outside the body, the infection is spread from person to person, i.e., by droplet infection. The saliva spray from an infected person while he is coughing or sneezing will reach to a distance of seven feet. The infection may also be carried by dust particles. Spitting on the streets is a dangerous practice. A third method of infection is through the use of handkerchiefs, towels, cups, and other objects contaminated by the fresh secretions. . . . In a serious attack, there is always a complicating infection in throat or lungs.

E. T. Hsieh, MD, DPH, "The Recent Epidemic of Influenza in Peking," *Zhonghua yi xue za zhi (The National Medical Journal)* XXII (1918): 129–32.

3

WILLIAM COLLIER

A New Type of Influenza

October 23, 1918

The Lancet *is a medical journal published in Great Britain. In the early days of the pandemic, its pages were filled with articles and letters concerning the unusual nature of the influenza. The following letter, from Dr. William Collier of Oxford, offers vivid examples of the variety of bewildering symptoms flu patients presented to him in his practice.*

To the Editor of *The Lancet*

Sir, — Surely we are seeing a type of influenza quite different from anything we have seen before. Side by side with influenza of the ordinary type we are meeting with cases which exhibit the following symptoms and physical signs. Within a few hours of seizure the patient's temperature runs up to 105° or over, while the pulse ranges round 90; a high temperature with a slow pulse; the lips and face exhibit marked cyanosis [blueness of the skin], and epistaxis [nosebleed] frequently occurs. In the course of a day or two the patient begins to spit up a quantity of frothy sputum tinged with bright blood. . . . For the first day or two the physical signs in the lungs are very indefinite and point to capillary bronchitis rather than to a broncho-pneumonia; later on there may develop signs of patches of consolidation [of capillary bronchitis]. . . . On the post-mortem table . . . distinct areas of haemorrhage into the lung tissue were present. I well remember the severe epidemic in 1889–90, and attended a large number of cases, but the signs and symptoms to which I refer, and which have been exhibited by patients I have attended during the past few days, are quite new to me.

Are we dealing with a new organism or with the recognised organisms of influenza which have for some reason attained greater virulence?

William Collier, "A New Type of Influenza," *The Lancet*, October 26, 1918, 567.

4

K. IWAGAWA

On Epidemic Influenza among Japanese Children

April 17, 1920

A Japanese physician writing in The Japan Medical World, *Iwagawa noted that younger children and babies appeared to contract the disease less frequently and less seriously than did older children.*

The infection occurred quite indifferently among people of all the ages, and occupation. Among children, it occurred more remarkably in an older one than among the younger. In the suckling, it occurred far less frequently. All the cases had unanimously an alike symptom. It developed more severely as the age advances, the suckling being only slightly affected. Prognosis also went parallel with the symptom in regard to the ages.

K. Iwagawa, "On Epidemic Influenza among Children, Clinical Observation and a Case of Influenzal Meningitis," *The Nippon No Ikai (The Japan Medical World)* X, no. 16 (April 17, 1920): 334.

5

GREAT BRITAIN REGISTRAR-GENERAL

Age Distribution of Deaths Due to Influenza in Ireland

1919

The Registrar-General of England and Wales, and its counterpart for Scotland and Ireland, have been responsible for keeping track of population statistics — births, deaths, and marriages — in Great Britain since the 1830s. In 1919, it issued a comprehensive report on the incidence of death resulting from influenza. These charts demonstrate the effect of the pandemic on various age cohorts in Ireland.

Great Britain Registrar-General, *Report on the Pandemic of Influenza, 1919* (London, 1919), 53.

Ireland—Deaths from Influenza at Age Periods

YEAR	SEX	UNDER FIVE YEARS	5–15	15–25	25–35	35–45	45–55	55–65	65–75	75 AND UPWARDS	TOTAL ALL AGES
1918	Males	625	431	1,205	1,390	706	448	317	321	148	5,591
1900	Males	257	64	86	92	122	202	418	528	437	2,206
1892	Males	306	75	97	86	112	198	305	358	294	1,831
1918	Females	621	533	997	1,032	579	427	321	373	177	5,060
1900	Females	238	69	106	78	103	257	534	622	464	2,471
1892	Females	241	93	122	85	98	204	357	417	294	1,911
1918	Males and Females	1,246	964	2,202	2,422	1,285	875	638	694	325	10,651
1900	Males and Females	495	133	192	170	225	459	952	1,150	901	4,677
1892	Males and Females	547	168	219	171	210	402	662	775	588	3,742

Proportion PER CENT. of Total Deaths

YEAR	SEX	UNDER FIVE YEARS	5–15	15–25	25–35	35–45	45–55	55–65	65–75	75 AND UPWARDS	TOTAL ALL AGES
1918	Males	11·2	7·7	21·6	24·8	12·6	8·0	5·7	5·8	2·6	100
1900	Males	11·8	2·8	3·9	4·2	5·5	9·2	18·9	23·9	19·8	100
1892	Males	16·7	4·1	5·3	4·7	6·1	10·8	16·7	19·6	16·0	100
1918	Females	12·3	10·5	19·7	20·4	11·4	8·4	6·4	7·4	3·5	100
1900	Females	9·6	2·8	4·3	3·2	4·2	10·4	21·6	25·2	18·7	100
1892	Females	12·5	4·9	6·4	4·5	5·1	10·7	18·7	21·8	15·4	100
1918	Males and Females	11·8	9·0	20·7	22·7	12·1	8·2	6·0	6·5	3·0	100
1900	Males and Females	10·6	2·8	4·1	3·6	4·8	9·8	20·4	24·6	19·3	100
1892	Males and Females	14·6	4·5	5·8	4·6	5·6	10·7	17·7	20·7	15·8	100

Ireland—Proportion per cent. of Deaths at Age Periods from Influenza and Pneumonia

YEAR	CAUSE OF DEATH	UNDER 5 YEARS	5–15	15–25	25–35	35–45	45–55	55–65	65–75	75 AND UPWARDS	TOTAL
1918	Influenza	11·8	9·0	20·7	22·7	12·1	8·2	6·0	6·5	3·0	100
1900	Influenza	10·6	2·8	4·1	3·6	4·8	9·8	20·4	24·6	19·3	100
1892	Influenza	14·6	4·5	5·8	4·6	5·6	10·7	17·7	20·7	15·8	100
1918	Pnemonia	28·8	7·1	11·6	13·0	8·7	8·4	8·1	9·2	5·1	100
1900	Pnemonia	23·5	4·1	5·7	7·8	10·8	11·7	16·4	12·8	7·2	100
1892	Pnemonia	17·4	5·3	6·7	7·0	9·9	14·2	17·9	13·8	7·8	100
1917	All causes	15·8	3·4	5·5	5·6	6·7	8·2	11·0	19·6	24·2	100

6

E. OLIVER ASHE

Some Random Recollections of the Influenza Epidemic in Kimberley, South Africa

January 11, 1919

The South African Medical Record *carried regular reports of the effects of influenza on patients. Here, a London doctor describes his experience treating patients at a hospital in Kimberley, South Africa, noting the marked difference between the virus of 1918–1919 and previous epidemics. It provides one of few accounts that mentions the effect of the disease on women's reproductive health, especially in pregnant women. Ashe also notes the prevalence and severity of the disease among native peoples and ponders whether the conditions in the Kimberley mines might be the cause of such disproportionate mortality rates.*

Having worked through epidemics in London (Whitechapel), Sheffield, and Maidstone nearly 30 years ago, I thought I knew what epidemic influenza meant; and when rumours of an impending outbreak began, I merely looked forward to a few weeks of extra hard work, with a rather heavy death-rate amongst the old, the feeble, and the alcoholic, though the majority of the cases would be mild.

But the avalanche that fell upon us, with its special mortality amongst robust people in the prime of life, who should theoretically have stood the disease best, was something very different. . . .

The severe cases were of two types: In one the main features were acute onset, rapid feeble pulse without specially high temperature, marked blueness of lips and nails, rather rapid breathing with chest pain or oppression, practically no cough and expectoration, an anxious expression, and great mental anxiety, but no discoverable lung affection. This type was invariably fatal, and the end came quickly. . . . In the other type the onset was less acute, and the early symptoms were not so severe, though the temperature ran higher (103° to 105° F.) from the

---

E. Oliver Ashe, "Some Random Recollections of the Kimberley Influenza Epidemic," *South African Medical Record,* January 11, 1919, 6–8.

start. Catarrhal symptoms, slight at first, soon become prominent, and after two or three days the expectoration became tinged with blood, pain developed somewhere in the chest, and consolidation . . . of some part of the lung could be found. . . . The cough became more troublesome, accompanied by the expectoration of large quantities of thin, slightly frothy, red fluid. . . .

Haemorrhage from the nose, mouth, and throat was common, and a few cases passed blood by the bowel.

Menstruation often came on too soon, lasted too long, and was too profuse, and this menstrual disturbance lasted for a period or two after convalescence. Pregnancy in the middle months did not seem to be disturbed, but abortion or premature labour was very liable to happen in the early and late months, and both of these put the patient into serious danger, more in the later than the earlier months, not a few women dying after premature labour. Severe and intractable vomiting occurred in a few of my fatal cases. . . .

Sleeplessness was an almost invariable symptom in the severe cases, and delirium, often violent, was common. . . .

The after-effects of the disease seemed endless, and there were few who did not find that they were a long time in shaking off the feeling of lassitude and debility, and keen business men complained that they could not concentrate their thoughts on their work; or remember business details with anything like their usual accuracy. . . .

The epidemic abounded in tragedies, of which, perhaps, the greatest was the appalling mortality amongst the natives in the compounds. Having had nothing to do with the native work myself, I have said nothing about it, but the acuteness of the attack, the extraordinary rapidity of its progress, and the terrible death-rate were matters of common knowledge. Why the natives should have been hit so hard is an unsolved problem. Was it just because natives always stand epidemic diseases badly, having no inherited immunity, or because the type of infection was severe, or because it became virulent from concentration in the underground chambers of the mines where they worked, and where, in spite of free ventilation, there must inevitably be some deficiency of pure air? A point worth noting in view of the last arguments is that the mortality amongst the white underground employees in the two mines most affected was 24 per cent.

7

MARY E. WESTPHAL

On Visiting Nurse Services in Chicago

November 8, 1918

Mary Westphal served as an Assistant Superintendent in the Visiting Nurse Association of Chicago. She and her colleagues ventured right into the heart of the epidemic, treating in their homes patients who had no means of getting themselves to hospitals or of paying for treatment. Her account offers a vivid picture of what daily life during the epidemic looked and felt like.

Because of bad housing conditions and over-crowding, we were very hard hit on the west side of Chicago, and are still getting calls where entire families are ill. Dirty streets, dirty alleys and just as dirty houses, and lack of proper sleeping quarters have made our work more than usually difficult.

The Ghetto was a hotbed of influenza and pneumonia. . . . The houses in this area are very close together and many families live under one roof. The people watched at their doors and windows, beckoning for the nurse to come in. One day a nurse who started out with fifteen patients to see saw nearly fifty before night. In District 28, where the streets are narrow and the people many, sixty-five calls were made in one day, though of course not all by one nurse. Fourteen calls in a busy season is a fair average for this small district. The Visiting Nurse repeatedly started out in the morning with a definite list of calls in her hand, but sometimes before getting out of her first case, she was surrounded by people asking her to go with them to see other patients. Physicians could not get around to all of the people needing them, it was impossible to get orders, consequently the nurse had to try to be many things to all people.

At first the gowns and masks which all of the nurses wore frightened the people, and several times women helpers who had come in

---

Mary E. Westphal, "Influenza Vignettes," *The Public Health Nurse* 11, no. 2 (1919): 129–33.

to stay left the homes on seeing the nurses so dressed up. Gradually they became accustomed to them and in many homes we trained the husband, or wife, or whoever was supplementing our care to the sick, to wear the gowns and masks.

On one of the coldest, rainiest days which we had, the nurse met on the sidewalk in front of a home, an eight-year-old boy, barefooted and in his nightdress. She quickly saw that he was delirious and coaxing him back into the house, she found the father sitting beside the stove, his head in his hands, two children in one bed, the mother and a two-weeks-old baby in another. She questioned the man, who was nearly crazed because, as he told her, he had just given his sick wife, a pneumonia patient, a spoonful of camphorated oil instead of castor oil. He had been up night and day caring for the wife and children, all with temperatures above 104, and his temperature at that time was 101.6. The nurse sent for the doctor, administered to the woman, bathed all of the patients, and sent the youngest child to the hospital, where he died a few days later. Several days afterwards, while the nurse was in the home, the mother had a severe hemorrhage from the ear. When we returned for our second call that same day we found that the patient, between our two visits, had been to the cemetery to see the child buried. With the exception of the one child, all in this family recovered. . . .

In one of our families the mother, father and two children had pneumonia at the same time. The father, in attempting to get up and help his wife, had fainted and fallen on the floor, and that was the way the nurse found him on her first visit. We made two daily calls and kept two aids [*sic*] there for a week, and all recovered.

In another district we found a man and his wife, both under thirty, fine, strong-looking, both ill with pneumonia. In another bed in the same room were two children under three with whooping cough and influenza. They were living in furnished rooms and had recently come here from another town. The man was wildly delirious from the start. We got them into separate rooms there and tried to make hospital arrangements, but were told that while there were empty beds at the three hospitals which we called, there were no nurses, so we had to keep the patients at home. We put a special nurse and an aid [*sic*] on, and the Visiting Nurse helped out by calling twice daily and assisting with the care. In spite of this, we lost both mother and father. The mother gave birth to an eight-months baby the day before she died; she lived eight hours after her husband. Both grandmothers came and each took one of the two older children, and placed the premature baby in the hospital.

Four of our families lost both mothers and fathers. We tried so hard to save a twenty-eight-year-old mother of four children, with a baby nine months old. She was pregnant and died on the eleventh day. This is a district of pretty comfortable homes, with no real poverty. . . .

In one of our Polish families we lost five out of one family of seven. . . . In one of our Jewish families, when the Visiting Nurse went to give care to a newly delivered mother one morning she found that a child two years old had died during the night. It was only by promising the mother that she could have the baby's body again that we could get it away from her, and she insisted upon having the little casket where she could see it until it was carried away. The mother made a good recovery.

In one of our Bohemian families six people living in three basement rooms were ill. . . . Many of our pregnant mothers died; some newly delivered mothers recovered, one young mother, twin delivery, who developed pneumonia on the third day, made an uneventful recovery. In the majority of our families most of the members were ill. Our patients were untouched until the nurse could get back to them, and each new case seemed more urgent than the last.

8

ANNE L. COLON

Influenza at Cedar Branch Camp, Michigan

1919

A registered nurse in Newberry, Michigan, Colon journeyed to northern Michigan to treat flu victims in a logging camp. Her report demonstrates that the disease did not confine itself to big cities, but spread into even the most remote areas of any given country.

Shall I tell you about how we took care of the influenza in a logging camp in the deep woods of northern Michigan, of the difficulty we had in reaching our patients, and what we accomplished?

Anne L. Colon, RN, "Experiences during the Epidemic, I: Influenza at Cedar Branch Camp," *American Journal of Nursing* 19, no. 8 (1919): 605–6.

No, our big cedar and balsam and hardwood forests, our fresh breezes from the Great Lakes, and our isolation from the crowded districts did not save us from the deadly grip of the epidemic. We read about the big cities, the suffering, and the many deaths, but still sat back; so fearless were we, and so sure of our wonderful healthy climate, that it wasn't until a cry for help came, that we were awakened from our dream.

Our first trip was to Cedar Branch, a camp fifteen miles in the woods. . . . Cedar Branch is a typical logging camp composed of a group of log cabins and tar paper shacks, all built near together in a friendly sort of way. The people are a fearless, careless, wandering tribe, followers of the great out-of-doors with little idea as to home-making and not any conception of sanitation. They have large families which usually live in a one-roomed cabin.

I shall never forget the conditions we found. Influenza was traveling like wildfire through the little huts. There was confusion, suffering, and terror everywhere. The sick and well were all huddled together. In many cases the family had only one bed, so we used rough heavy cloth, sewed the four sides, slit one side in the middle, these we filled with straw and used for extra beds. There was a roaring fire in each house, the windows were nailed down, and the doors shut tight. The people were afraid of a bit of fresh air, and it took a good deal of tact, and in some cases force, to get air to them. Another of our greatest difficulties was to stop their careless spitting on the walls, on the floor, and everywhere. The way we did check it was to place a tin can on a chair beside each bed and make them use them. These cans were burned each day and fresh ones given. At camps they use a great deal of canned food, so one can always find a good supply of them. We could not get to camp every day, but during our absence we left several responsible women to see that all went well. We saw to it that these women were well instructed, for life and death hung in the balance.

Altogether we had between forty and fifty cases at Cedar Branch, and we lost only one thirteen-months-old baby; that was a better record than at many of the neighboring camps.

9

IJIRO GOMIBUCHI

Personal Account of the World Influenza Epidemic

May 1919

A doctor serving a rural community in the Yaita district of Japan, some 80 miles north of Tokyo, Ijiro Gomibuchi published an account of his experiences with influenza patients. At first he attributed the lethality of the epidemic to a form of diphtheria, but in the course of his practice he came to believe that it was due to pneumonia. In the following passage, he describes a typical day during the worst weeks of the pandemic, from mid-November through the end of December 1918.

It started snowing about 10 o'clock in the morning of 11 December, and I had received a request to go out to two houses in Anzawa early that morning. I set off on my bicycle not long after it started snowing. On the way I visited and treated two households with influenza cases, so it was 2 P.M. before I reached Anzawa. Most of the houses were shuttered against the snow, so it all felt quiet and desolate. I noticed a rickshaw parked under the eaves of one house, and guessed that a doctor was there visiting a patient. When I got to one of the stricken houses that had called for me, I found that the young bride had caught the flu two or three days previously. She was pregnant, and had miscarried and died. Because the family were all sick, the young woman's own family had had to arrange her funeral. Now the 39-year-old wife of the householder had developed pneumonia. For the past several days, all the doctors had joined in treating her. . . . I saw her, and I guessed that she wouldn't last out the night. Then I went to the other house to which I'd been called. . . . After that I treated people in eight other households.

By now it was getting dark. I set off homeward in the snow on foot about 7 P.M. On the way I passed a little liquor bar, and could see the

---

Translation of Dr. Ijiro Gomibuchi's *Personal Account of the World Influenza Epidemic of 1918–19, with Remarks on the Use of Diphtheria Serum* (May 1919), trans. Edwina Palmer and Geoffrey W. Rice, in "A Japanese Physician's Response to Pandemic Influenza: Ijiro Gombuchi and the 'Spanish Flu' in Yaita-Cho, 1918–1919," *Bulletin of the History of Medicine* 66 (1992): 569–70, 573.

lights through the *shōji* [paper windows], and I could smell the *sake* and hear the chatter and laughter inside. It set my mouth watering! But being a doctor I am forbidden these things, so I trudged by in the snow. A bit further along, in the snow by the roadside, I came upon the rickshaw I had noticed previously. The rickshaw puller had collapsed in the snow. Thinking nothing of my own safety, but only of saving the patient, I carried him back to a household I knew would be willing to look after him. The house where I first saw the rickshaw now had its shutters open, and I could see people silhouetted against the paper windows. The flu sufferer there had died, and already the neighbors were gathering around, mourning.

I walked on another 300 meters or so through a wood, and passed a Buddhist temple surrounded by its cemetery, looking desolate and sad. There was no sound in the snow. I cannot describe how my blood ran cold at the sudden wailing of a woman who was calling to her dying husband. To judge by that, a fourth person would die during the night, to add to the three who had died in the village that day.

I got home about 8 o'clock that evening. The girl Akuzu Yasu, whom we employed as a child-minder, had come down with flu on 28 November, and had developed pneumonia. She was in critical condition. I had been treating her, but already her pulse was weak. I spent that night giving her injections, but next morning she died pitifully. She was only fifteen. Previously I had thought of giving her injections of diphtheria serum, but since she was not my own child I could not, because it would be like experimenting on a human guinea pig. If only I had, I might have prolonged her life for a few days, or even just saved her, and now I kicked myself that I had not tried these injections sooner.

. . . I realized now that there were so many patients that there were not enough doctors to treat them all. In the past, there had always been enough doctors to treat the sick in this district.

. . . Those who conduct the funeral service, and people in the neighborhood, all catch it, because they all help each other and don't think about catching it, and so they die.

10

JOSIE MABEL BROWN

Recollections of a U.S. Navy Nurse

1986

Born in 1886, Josie Mabel Brown completed her nursing training in 1917, just as the United States entered the Great War on the side of the Allies. She was drafted into the Nursing Corps as soon as she graduated. She left the Navy in September 1919 and worked as a nurse in a military school. In 1986 she gave the following interview to her niece, Rachel Wedeking.

How did you begin your Navy career?

One day I was at the theater and suddenly the screen went blank. Then a message appeared across the screen: "Would Josie M. Brown please report to the ticket office?" I went back and there was a Western Union boy with a telegram from the Bureau of Medicine and Surgery in Washington, DC. It said, "You are called to duty. Do you have enough money to travel? And when is the earliest date that you can travel?" And I wired back, "I have money. I can pay my way." About 45 minutes later a reply came back. "Proceed to Great Lakes, Illinois. Keep strict account of your expenses. Do not pay over $1.50 for your meals or over 50¢ for tips. You will be reimbursed."

My train was an old pullman going to Chicago. I went right through our town and saw the light in the window that mother put there. I got to Chicago in the morning. When someone opened a paper in front of me I saw "6,000 in the hospital have Spanish Influenza in Great Lakes, Illinois." I said, "Oh, that's where I'm going. What *is* Spanish Influenza?"

I got to the gate and showed my Red Cross pin and my orders. They put me on a bus and sent me to the main hospital, then took me for my first meal in the service. It was cold pork, sweet potatoes, and apple sauce. Afterward, my supervisor took me to a ward that was supposedly caring for 42 patients. There was a man lying on the bed dying and one was lying on the floor. Another man was on a stretcher waiting for the fellow on the bed to die. We would wrap him in a winding sheet because

---

Rachel Wedeking interview with Josie Mabel Brown, in "A Winding Sheet and a Wooden Box," *Navy Medicine* 77, No. 3 (May–June 1986): 18–19. Reprinted by permission.

he had stopped breathing. I don't know whether he was dead or not, but we wrapped him in a winding sheet and left nothing but the big toe on the left foot out with a shipping tag on it to tell the man's rank, his nearest of kin, and hometown. And the ambulance carried four litters. It would bring us four live ones and take out four dead ones.

Did they keep them in the morgue?

The morgues were packed almost to the ceiling with bodies stacked one on top of another. The morticians worked day and night. You could never turn around without seeing a big red truck being loaded with caskets for the train station so the bodies could be sent home.

Was there any treatment for these boys?

We didn't have time to treat them. We didn't take temperatures; we didn't even have time to take blood pressure.

What did you do for the temperature?

We would give them a little hot whiskey toddy; that's about all we had time to do. They would have terrific nosebleeds with it. Sometimes the blood would just shoot across the room. You had to get out of the way or someone's nose would bleed all over you.

What other symptoms did they have?

Some were delirious and some had their lungs punctured. Then their bodies would fill with air. You would feel somebody and he would be bubbles.

That must have been a terrible disease.

You would see them with bubbles all through their arms.

You mean air would get into their tissues?

Yes. Oh, it was a horrid thing. We had to wear operating masks and gowns all the time. We worked 8 hours on a ward sometimes. If nobody had a nurse on another ward, we would go back to our quarters for an hour and then work another 8 hours. It was 16 hours a day until the epidemic was over.

When was that?

The worst was over just a little before Christmas 1918. I was assigned to another ward by that time. One day a man came through and said the armistice was signed. The boys just about hit the ceiling they were so glad. During the epidemic, though, our Navy bought the whole city of

Chicago out of sheets. There wasn't a sheet left in Chicago. All a boy got when he died was a winding sheet and a wooden box; we just couldn't get enough caskets.

I understand you also caught the flu.

It was March 1919 when I got sick. They didn't have a room for me so they curtained me off in a ward with other women. They didn't know what I had because I was never diagnosed. I ran a temperature of 104° or 105° for days; I just don't remember how many days. They put an ice cap on my head, an ice collar on my neck, and an ice pack over my heart. My heart pounded so hard that it rattled the ice; everything was rattling, including the chartboard and bedsprings.

Did you have any idea how many died altogether?

They died by the thousands. There were 173,000 men at Great Lakes at the time, and 6,000 were in the hospitals at the height of the epidemic. I suppose no one knows how many died. They just lost track of them.

11

SIERRA LEONE WEEKLY NEWS

Coffins

October 26, 1918

The numbers of dead left by the flu vastly outpaced the ability of carpenters to produce sufficient numbers of coffins to bury them. This was true of every country overtaken by the pandemic. Here, a news item details the magnitude of the problem, as doctors, colonial officials, and bereaved families in Sierra Leone struggled to bury the dead.

The question of coffins was a most acute one. Very few if any boards were to be obtained in town and how to bury their dead gave more anxiety to bereaved families and friends than almost anything else. The Government had sometime before the outbreak notified the public that no

"Coffins," *Sierra Leone Weekly News*, October 26, 1918, 10.

coffins will be supplied in future by the P.W.D. [Public Works Department] owing to the scarcity of boards. The hour for burial was generally determined by the time a coffin could be obtained. Mats were used by the Medical Department for wrapping up the dead and all sorts of coverings were used by the native population who died in abnormal numbers.

Interment consequently took place at all hours of the day even after sunset and under all weathers. Many of the people at [the town of] Half Die took their dead at night and deposited them in the Hospital compound, and it was quite common for the medical staff to look after about ten or more corpses daily for which they could not account. Corpses were picked from all quarters of the town in the streets, and the whole place was a valley of the shadow of death.

12

SIR THOMAS HORDER

The Post-Febrile Period

December 28, 1918

A number of physicians and scientists emphasized the mental and emotional effects of the flu on their patients, many of whom suffered for long periods after the disease had passed. Here, a British physician describes the symptoms that followed the febrile, or fever, stage in an item for The Lancet.

In a large number of the severe cases, and in not a few of the mild ones, a state of exhaustion quite disproportionate to the duration of the illness follows the pyrexial [fever] period. Careful examination reveals no incriminating features in any organ. The degree of prostration may be profound, and may be much more trying both to patient and doctor than was the disease itself. . . . The "higher centres" suffer chiefly; marked depression is common, emotional instability is often seen, and suicide is

Thomas Horder, "Some Observations on the More Severe Cases of Influenza Occurring during the Present Epidemic," *The Lancet*, December 28, 1918, 871–73.

by no means rare. In a few cases a condition of amnesia which was present during the febrile stages persists for some days, then clears away. Neurasthenic states [mental and physical exhaustion] and insomnia which were present before the illness tend to be accentuated, or, if they were yielding to time and treatment when the disease appeared, they are prone afterwards to give further trouble.

13

A. HAY-MICHEL

Nervous Symptoms in Influenza Patients

January 25, 1919

Dr. A. Hay-Michel, a physician on the Zaaiplaats Mine in South Africa, speaks of the extraordinarily high fevers that flu patients ran and the delirium and hallucinations that accompanied them. As described in Document 12, mental symptoms continued to plague victims even after the disease had passed.

Nervous symptoms . . . began with acute maniacal attacks requiring physical restraint. . . . [The patient's] temperature rose to 107° F., and he had to be constantly in cold wet packs for two days before the temperature could be reduced for any length of time. He then . . . lay in a state of stupor for 24 hours, when he relapsed, his temperature again rising to 108° F. with acute and active delirium which lasted two days and was followed by a similar crisis, with great exhaustion and mental torpor. He subsequently had a second relapse, which, however, was much milder, finally making a complete recovery, though his mental state caused a good deal of anxiety for three weeks after his second relapse.

Neurasthenia, mental depression, various paraesthesiae and muscular weakness of loins and lower limbs have been common complaints during convalescence, irrespective of severity of attacks.

A. Hay-Michel, "Influenza on the Zaaiplaats Mine," *South African Medical Record*, January 25, 1919, 25.

2

Transmission and Mortality

14

SANTA FE MONITOR (KANSAS)

Early Reports of Influenza in the United States

January–February 1918

The Santa Fe Monitor *published what appear to be the first reports of the outbreak of the influenza epidemic, in Haskell County, Kansas, in late January and February 1918. By March, the disease would spread to Camp Funston (now Fort Riley, Kansas), a United States Army base situated three hundred miles east of Haskell, which was the destination of a number of Haskell boys who had enlisted in the military.*

January 24, 1918: Owen Nelson reports their baby on the mend. It has been quite sick with LaGrippe. . . . Mr. Earnest Dyerly south of town is quite sick with pneumonia.

February 7, 1918: A. W. Hensley, who recently had the measles, has contracted the pneumonia and is very sick. His father came in Tuesday from Wichita.

February 14, 1918: Mertin, the young son of Ernest Elliott, is sick with pneumonia but is getting along very nicely. . . . Audrey Burr, Raymond Murphy, Laura and Ralph Lindeman are among those in Sublette who are sick with pneumonia. . . . Homer Moody has been quite sick with pneumonia but is reported bet[ter]. The Girod baby is quite sick.

Santa Fe Monitor, January 24, 1918; February 7, 1918; February 14, 1918; February 21, 1918.

February 21, 1918: Mrs. Eva Van Alstine is sick with pneumonia. Her little son Roy is now able to be up. Mrs. Elmer Barlow brought her baby to Sublette Saturday evening for medical attention as it was quite sick. . . . Ralph McConnell has been quite sick this week. . . . Several school children have been absent this week on account of sickness. Most everybody over the country is having the lagrippe [*sic*] or pneumonia. Nina Alexander has been among the ailing list this week. . . . Several people of this neighborhood [Jean, Kansas] have been entertaining the lagrippe [*sic*] recently.

15

DAILY EXPRESS (LONDON)

Mystery Malady Spreading in the Large Towns of Sweden

May 30, 1918

The pandemic moved across the Atlantic on board troopships carrying members of the American Expeditionary Force to fight on behalf of the Allies. Here, the London Daily Express *briefly details the outbreak of influenza in Stockholm, Sweden.*

COPENHAGEN, WEDNESDAY, MAY 29. Several new cases of the "mystery malady" have been detected in Stockholm, and it is spreading particularly in the largest cities, where food conditions are very bad.

The malady is characterised by decreasing muscular strength, slow pulsation, and low temperature.

Men, women, and children are suffering from the disease.

"Mystery Malady," *Daily Express* (London), May 30, 1918, 2.

16

DAILY EXPRESS (LONDON)

The Mystery War Disease: Its Appearance in Belfast

June 13, 1918

This is the first notice of an outbreak of the disease in Great Britain. Though the illness is reported to be mild in its impact, at least one munitions factory closed down owing to the large number of workers who fell sick, most of whom were women.

BELFAST, WEDNESDAY. Belfast is at present in the throes of a mysterious epidemic, which in some respects resembles those in Spain and Scandinavia.

The medical authorities are of opinion that it is due to a microbe of an influenzal character. The symptoms include feverishness, headache, sore throat, and pains in the body. Many establishments have been affected by the epidemic, but up to the present only one has found it necessary to close down. This is a firm in which women munition workers are employed. The men employed by the firm are unaffected, but work is suspended for the week owing to the illness of women workers.

The premises have been fumigated and every precaution to prevent the malady from spreading is being taken. An outbreak was reported among soldiers in the city, and the patients have been quarantined.

Doctors say there is no cause for alarm. The patients are really suffering from an acute form of influenza, which, if properly treated, will disappear in the course of a few days. No deaths have been reported.

"The Mystery War Disease," *Daily Express* (London), June 13, 1918, 3.

17

DAILY EXPRESS (LONDON)

The New War Disease in Germany: Mystery Epidemic Now Ravaging Berlin, Doctors Powerless

June 17, 1918

Although wartime conditions prevented British reporters from issuing their stories directly from Germany, word of the spread of influenza to Berlin still made its way to British newspapers, likely through neutral countries. Here, the London Daily Express ***issues an early report.***

AMSTERDAM, SUNDAY, JUNE 16. The Berlin newspapers state that the German capital is now suffering from an acute epidemic of influenza, which, owing to the bad health conditions, is making alarmingly rapid progress.

It is stated that although the illness has every characteristic of influenza, it is coupled with extraordinarily strong fever and severe pain in the limbs, which give the disease an extremely disquieting character. The "Lokalanzeiger's" medical correspondent believes that the Berlin outbreak is very similar to that reported from Spain, and the number of cases is admitted to be very large.

In view of the fact that the people of Berlin are already greatly weakened by war privations, it is feared that Berlin's "Spanish influenza," as it is called, will have grave consequences, especially as no preventive measures have yet been devised against the illness.

"The New War Disease in Germany," *Daily Express* (London), June 17, 1918, 3.

18

PUBLIC HEALTH REPORTS

Influenza a Probable Cause of Fever of Undetermined Nature in Southern States

June 21, 1918

In early June, U.S. authorities reported an explosive outbreak of the disease at Fort Oglethorpe in Georgia. The U.S. Department of Public Health issued a bulletin warning of an outbreak across the southern states in June as well, indicating that the disease had moved from the military to the civilian population.

Fevers of an undetermined nature were reported during April and May at various points from Norfolk to Louisiana. An examination of the records and reports of the physicians who have treated these cases leads to the belief that these fevers were mainly influenza of mild type. It is possible, however, that all cases reported were not of the same disease, and in one locality in Louisiana dengue [fever] may have occurred.

Public Health Reports, Vol. 33, no. 25, June 21, 1918.

19

THE TIMES (LONDON)

Influenza Spreading in Germany

July 4, 1918

By July, reports coming through the Netherlands to Britain indicated that influenza in Germany had reached significant heights, despite efforts of German authorities to downplay the incidence. Because it was mistakenly thought to have originated in Spain, the disease was quickly dubbed "Spanish influenza" by the press.

THE HAGUE, JULY 3. "Spanish influenza" is increasing in Germany to an alarming extent. Many large industries in Berlin are suffering from the illness of their employees. In two weeks the number of patients on the books of the Berlin local sickness insurance office has increased from 16,000 to 18,000. From 200 to 300 new patients are reported daily.

In the greater part of Bavaria "Spanish influenza" prevails, and cases are increasing daily in Munich. The epidemic is also reported from Nuremberg, Regensberg, Passau, Ingolstadt, Landshut, and various other places. Fifty workwomen are suffering from influenza in the great factory of Nieder Sedlitz, near Dresden.

Another Berlin report says that a large number of patients suffering from influenza were received on Monday into the larger Berlin hospitals. The Charité rejected 50 slight cases and retained about 10. One whole department of the Charité, comprising some 30 beds, has been closed owing to the danger of infection. Another Berlin hospital admitted 35 influenza cases on Monday. The malady has caused many gaps among the workers employed in the public services. All the women clerks and other female employees in a branch of one big bank are incapacitated.

The Berlin Municipal medical authority reports that the malady is of quite a light character and there is no ground for uneasiness.

A Danzig telegram reports the appearance of the malady in the Danzig garrison hospital.

"Influenza Spreading in Germany," *The Times* (London), July 4, 1918, 5.

AMSTERDAM, JULY 3. — A Berlin telegram to the *Telegraaf* says that conferences have been held at Main Headquarters in which all the high Army medical authorities participated, to discuss means of preventing the spread of the epidemic to the front. The most energetic measures have been decided upon. — *Reuter.*

20

LAGOS STANDARD

Influenza in Lagos, Nigeria

October 2, 1918

By the time the pandemic reached Africa, the virus causing it had mutated, producing a much more virulent form of the disease than its initial manifestation. British colonial authorities in Nigeria, having learned from their experience in Sierra Leone how quickly the illness spread, responded with stern measures. The Lagos Standard, ***an anticolonial newspaper, condemned the authorities for following policies that had the effect of unnecessarily panicking the people of Lagos and increasing the spread of the disease.***

It is difficult to write with composure on the carryings on of the Sanitary Authorities the last few days in this town. The town has been thrown into a panic worse than Influenza itself. People are afraid even to be sick. Men, women and children dare not have fever, dare not cough or suffer from headache. The slightest rise of temperature is a symptom of Influenza and the offender must go either to the Infectious Diseases Hospital or the Quarantine Station at Abekun. In neither of these places we are creditably informed is there accommodation for the better class natives and the arrangements for food for the unfortunate people sent there are bad. Many people who had been to the Quarantine Station have complained of being made to sleep on bare cement floor or with only palm leaves on the floor to serve as mats. And many of these people

---

Editorial: "Influenza in Lagos," *Lagos Standard*, October 2, 1918.

have been compelled to leave their comfortable beds and good homes with good and abundant food to undergo as Influenza "contacts" the hardships both of want of food and physical discomfort and be exposed to conditions that might make them catch their deaths of cold. We are afraid the Sanitary Authorities have been too hasty in many of the methods they have advised Government to adopt for the control of the present epidemic of Influenza. The hastiness in enforcing regulations which are impracticable have [*sic*] resulted in creating panic in the town. As we have said people are now in mortal dread and many to escape being sent to Isolation Hospitals where they are exposed to dampness and cold and insufficient and[,] to many[,] unaccustomed food of cheap quality have avoided the railway and fled to the country. Luckily the type of Influenza that is prevalent in the town at present is not virulent or else the disease will have spread to and played havoc in the country and it will have been a very difficult job to eradicate it. As a matter of fact we think that the Sanitary Authorities have been attempting too much. It is a very big job to undertake the isolation of people infected by Influenza raging as an epidemic in a population of 80,000. No public authority would attempt such a thing in an infectious disease like Influenza which spreads rapidly from place to place or in a town. We think the situation will have been met and aptly met too if the authorities had stopped at the closing of the schools, the issuing of instructions for the guidance of the people and the Medical Officer of Health had spent his energy in advising Medical practitioners as to the proper method of isolating patients in their homes and pursuing his usual sanitary duties with respect to the cleaning of the town, keeping ever watchful eyes on the general death-rate, the movements of passengers and steamers and behaving generally in such a way as to make the people confident and free from panic.

21

J. A. ODUENADE

Spreading Influenza to the Nigerian Countryside

October 28, 1918

In a letter to the editor of the Lagos Standard, *this correspondent signaled that the epidemic had already made its way into the Nigerian hinterland and threatened to do tremendous damage to the populations of the interior.*

Referring to the article under "Influenza" in your paper of the 23rd instant which is up to the point I respectfully beg to hint that you will also be rendering invaluable services to the race by calling attention of the authorities, to the fact that as the epidemic has played such a great havoc in a place like Lagos with its age and growth of enlightenment and advantages too numerous to enumerate, early precautionary measures are essential to protect our people in the hinterland where the mere words of advice as to symptoms and modes of living peculiar to the desease [*sic*] if sympathetically preached by government Representative and strictly seen adhered to would rescue them from the dreadful devastation of the plague and the barbarous treatment with the native medicene [*sic*] in which about 95% of us have hereditary faith. Perhaps a Travelling Doctor &c &c may be spared for this purpose. Staggering news have been received from some important centres up country — and it is feared if timely steps are not taken the epidemic may create a reign of terror with its unbridled virulence.

J. A. Oduenade, letter to the editor, dated October 28, 1918, in the *Lagos Standard*, October 30, 1918.

22

M. CAMERON BLAIR AND J. BERINGER

Report on the Influenza Outbreak, Nigeria

September 5, 1919

M. Cameron Blair and J. Beringer served as Sanitary Officers in the British colony of Nigeria, which was administratively broken into the Northern and Southern Provinces. They submitted their reports in response to the Colonial Office's efforts to gain an understanding of the scope of the pandemic and the ability of colonial officers to deal with the upheaval it caused.

In the middle of September, 1918, a telegram was received from Lagos, from the Senior Sanitary Officer, Southern Provinces, to the effect that Influenza had been declared an Infectious Disease there, and that six cases, from three ships from Sierra Leone and the Gold Coast, had already been isolated. On the 21st of the same month, a Reuter's telegram was received, at Kaduna, giving an alarming account of the ravages being perpetrated at Sierra Leone by the visitation. . . .

The invasion made it's [*sic*] way steadily into the Northern Provinces along the easiest avenues and by the most expeditious means of transport, to wit:

(a), by the Railway, (b), by the rivers which were then high, and (c), by the overland trade routes. All through, the invasion made it's [*sic*] progress at the normal speed of travel; whether by rail, by steamer, by canoe, or by foot-travel. . . .

After Lagos and the towns on the railway, the next place known to be infected was Calabar at the eastern end of the coast line of Nigeria. A native was removed to Hospital from the S.S. Batanga on the 28th September but not diagnosed as Influenza but the subsequent conclusion was that it must have been a case of this disease "although no cases suspicious of Influenza were reported as having occurred on the Batanga." Isolated shore cases began to appear on and after the 7th October: they

---

M. Cameron Blair, "Pandemic of Influenza: Experience in the Northern Provinces of Nigeria"; J. Beringer, "The Influenza Epidemic of 1918 in the Southern Provinces of Nigeria," ***Influenza Outbreak.*** Great Britain, Colonial Office, CO 583/77, C202208.

were mild and occurred amongst the Marine and Customs Departments and the Shipping Company's employees clearly pointing to infection by ocean ship; they gradually became more numerous and more severe until "on the 14th and 15th of November there came a sudden outburst with hundreds of cases." . . .

The primary focus of infection for the whole of the Southern Provinces was Lagos and . . . spread took place through native river and road traffic. Infection did radiate from these two ports [Calabar and Forcados] and no doubt would eventually have involved the whole of Nigeria but actually its arrival from these sources was forestalled for the most part by its more rapid progress by river and road routes from Lagos, directly or indirectly. . . .

The rapidity with which the disease spread was remarkable. . . . Spread was much facilitated by natives running away from infected places and so carrying the disease with them. In Port Harcourt for instance nearly 1000 labourers deserted and returned to their own districts whilst the Resident of the Onitsha Province states that November is the month during which according to Native Custom the people of this part of the country must return home or pay a fine; this movement of large numbers from all over Nigeria no doubt greatly assisted the dissemination of the Epidemic.

23

THE TIMES (LONDON)

Cape Town in the Grip of Influenza

October 10, 1918

The South African correspondent for The Times *of London drew attention to the fact that the flu hit indigenous and Indian populations in the industrial and urban centers of the country far more severely than it did white settlers (see also Document 6). He also reported on the rumor that poison gas used by the Germans on the western front had caused the disease.*

"Cape Town in the Grip of Influenza," *The Times* (London), October 10, 1918, 5.

CAPE TOWN, OCT. 6. The epidemic currently called "Spanish influenza" is assuming the proportions of a national calamity. Kimberley and Johannesburg have both been swept by the disease, and Cape Town is now in the full grip of the malady, which is attacking with special virulence and alarming results the coloured and native communities. It is believed to have been imported from Sierra Leone.

The scenes in Cape Town are unprecedented. It is estimated that fully 14,000 cases, drawn from all classes, are compelling the complete or partial suspension of activities of all kinds. The town is noticeably empty, the medical and nursing services are crippled, and even the food supplies are presenting difficulties; while in the poorer quarters terrible distress prevails, whole families being completely prostrated in the absence of medical aid.

A high medical authority states that the disease is directly related to the German use of poison gas, the after-effects of which have induced the growth of a new type of streptococcus, which has now been isolated.

24

C. E. L. BURMAN

A Review of the Influenza Epidemic in Rural South Africa

January 11, 1919

Rural locales in South Africa also showed a disproportionate mortality rate among indigenous peoples, as this report in the South African Medical Record *indicates. White Afrikaner farmers and their families fared better than native Africans, though they displayed the same peculiar pattern of age-related mortality.*

C. E. L. Burman, "A Review of the Influenza Epidemic in Ladysmith and District, with Clinical Observations," *South African Medical Record,* January 11, 1919, 3–6.

Sporadic cases of influenza were recognized in Ladysmith and District towards the end of August, but it was not until the first week in October that it attained epidemic form. From the 10th October to 22nd October the epidemic was at its height, affecting more or less 85 per cent. of the population in Ladysmith, and, from reports, nearly 70 per cent. of the District. The districts of Umhlumayo, Wessels Nek, Matawana's Kop, Modder Spruit, and Roseboam — all Native locations — were those most severely attacked, Ladysmith itself receiving the severest blow.

The farms and kraals [corrals] bordering on the main road to Bergville, Elandslaagte, Matawana and Van Reenen areas, although affected, did not suffer to the same extent as those already mentioned. The mortality amongst the natives has been due in very many cases to their own methods of treatment, want of food, inability to cope with the situation, and neglect on their part to carry out instructions when given to them, pneumonia, heart failure and exhaustion being the chief causes of death. The mortality amongst the white population in the district has not been heavy, possibly due to the simple methods of treatment adopted which were found so beneficial in the town itself, but only after the epidemic had taken a heavy toll. The disease showed a marked affinity for adults, and amongst them the mortality was heaviest and the type severe. Children and grown-ups over 50 as a rule caused little anxiety.

25

BRITISH MEDICAL JOURNAL

Influenza in India

April 5, 1919

The British Medical Journal *reported on the massive death toll caused by the flu in 1918 and 1919, though the figures turn out to be wildly underestimated.*

"Influenza in India," *British Medical Journal,* April 5, 1919, 417.

The preliminary report on the influenza epidemic by Major Norman White, I.M.S., Sanitary Commissioner with the Government of India, carries the story down to November 30th, 1918. . . . In the middle of September the Bombay death-rate began to rise, and the second wave of influenza, which reached its crest in October, caused a havoc to which the Black Death of 1348–49 alone affords a parallel. . . . Not fewer than 4,899,725 persons (about 2 per cent. of the whole population) died of influenza or its complications in British India, the vast majority within the space of two months. Making allowance for the native states, not less than six million persons perished in India. . . .

The explanation suggested for this enormous death roll is that Indians have a low resisting power to pneumonic infection. . . . It would appear from the military data that the fatality rate for Indian troops was at least three times that found amongst British troops in India. . . . Another factor was a scarcity of food grains, and especially of fodder, which was responsible for a dearth of milk, both being results of the failure of the monsoon.

26

WILLIAM W. CADBURY

The 1918 Pandemic of Influenza in Canton

January 1920

Dr. William W. Cadbury, an American physician at the University Medical School in Canton, China, reports that the country appears to have suffered far less from mortality due to influenza than the rest of the world. He notes the contrast to the incidence of mortality with other nations, including the United States, the Philippines, and most notably India, where famine reigned.

William W. Cadbury, "The 1918 Pandemic of Influenza in Canton," *China Medical Journal* (January 1920): 15–16.

It is estimated that in September, October, and November [1918], there were more than 400,000 deaths from the disease in America. Among the troops, from September 20 to November 1 there were reported 725 deaths from influenza, and 18,704 from pneumonia. In the cities of America the death rate ranged from 1.8 per thousand in Milwaukee, to 7.4 per thousand in Philadelphia for a period of ten weeks. At the Christian College [in Canton] only one death occurred between June and January, or a rate of one per thousand for the three epidemics. Elsewhere in Canton the disease seems to have been very much less malignant than in the United States, although there were rumors of entire families being wiped out, and of 500 deaths having occurred in one block of a city street. At the Canton Hospital there were no deaths in June, and only four among 27 cases in October.

Rumors indicate that the disease was much more fatal in certain outlying districts of Canton, but the reports from Hongkong and Shanghai agree with our own observations that the death rate was extremely low in China. That tropical countries did suffer severely from the disease is shown by [reports from] the Philippines and by recent despatches from India stating that the deaths there ran up into the millions. As Christian emphasizes, it is a misnomer to speak of some deaths as being due to influenza and others as due to pneumonia, since death is practically always caused by pneumonia.

27

GRESHAM LIFE ASSURANCE SOCIETY

Influenza Claims Exceed War Claims

July 1, 1919

A British insurance company reported at its annual meeting that despite the high volume of claims it had to pay out in 1918 owing to a huge increase in mortality, it nevertheless managed to turn a profit.

Gresham Life Assurance Society (Limited), "A Progressive Year. Influenza Claims Exceed War Claims," *The Times* (London), July 1, 1919, 22.

[The] death claims brought into account during the year [1918] amount to an abnormally large sum and show an exceptionally large increase upon the figures for 1917. . . . The total war claims from 1914 to 1918 inclusive . . . amount to no less a sum than £190,000. . . .

It may interest you to know that the death claims from the fatal scourge of influenza, which last year so rapidly spread over all parts of the world, have, in our experience at any rate, exceeded considerably the war claims of the year. These, likewise, are obviously included. But, gentlemen, it affords myself and my colleagues great pleasure to be able to state to you that, large as are the death claims reported, it is our duty and our pleasure now to report that they are nevertheless, as we are advised by the actuary, within the actuarial expectation. (Hear, hear). Obviously the margin cannot be a great one, but it is gratifying to know that, notwithstanding the exceptional conditions of the year — the accumulation of the past and the influenza — we are on the safety side of the line.

3
Treatment Responses

28

VICTORIA (AUSTRALIA) BOARD OF PUBLIC HEALTH

"Spanish" Influenza

November 23, 1918

T. W. H. Holmes, the Secretary of the Victoria Board of Public Health in Australia, issued a detailed set of directives to the public informing them of the symptoms, treatment, spread, and prevention of influenza. His bulletin differed from that of many other countries in its inclusion of the legal requirements imposed on citizens who contracted the disease.

"Spanish" influenza is ordinary influenza associated with germs which cause pneumonia.

Symptoms. — The onset is generally sudden, beginning with a chill or a shivering fit and high fever. Headache and backache ensue, followed by a general aching of the body, and extreme weakness. Sometimes the disease begins with reddening and running of the eyes, coughing, sneezing, and sore throat.

Occasionally the attack is ushered in by —

(a) Vomiting and diarrhea, accompanied by severe abdominal pains; or

(b) A sudden faint; or

T. W. H. Holmes, "Board of Public Health, Victoria (Australia). 'Spanish' Influenza Notice." In Niall Johnson, *Britain and the 1918–19 Influenza Pandemic: A Dark Epilogue* (London: Routledge, 2006), 134–35.

(c) An epileptiform fit; or
(d) Symptoms of acute mania; or
(e) Delirium tremens

Complications. — The most important and the most dangerous complication of influenza is pneumonia. The presence of pneumonia is revealed by high fever, flushed face, cough, increased frequency and difficulty of breathing, and sharp pains in the chest.

Treatment. — Bed should be sought at the onset of symptoms. Complete rest is the best way to prevent complications. Plenty of food and water should be taken. Quinine, salicylates, acetylsalicylic acid, and phenacetin have proved to be the most useful drugs in relieving symptoms. They do not, however, prevent or cure influenza. Air and light should freely enter the room. Owing to the dangerous complications that may follow even a mild case of influenza, medical advice should be obtained early.

How influenza is spread. — The infecting organisms are contained in the discharges from the mouth and nose; hence the disease is spread by transmission of these germs from the infected to the healthy. The commonest way in which the disease is contracted is by inhaling small particles of infected sputum or nasal mucus expelled in the act of coughing or sneezing. Infection is also acquired by medium of common towels, cups, glasses, and any other article soiled with infected discharges.

Prevention. —

(1) Isolation of patients and contacts.
(2) Disinfection of discharges from mouth and nose of patients and contacts.
(3) Disinfection of nose and mouth cavities by douches, mouth washes, sprays, and inhalations.
(4) Attendants on patients and contacts should wear a gauze mask or suitable respirator.
(5) Avoid crowds; be in the open air as much as possible. Allow sunshine and air to freely enter all living, sleeping, and working rooms. Avoid fatigue, and beware of the cougher and sneezer.
(6) Evidence from South Africa shows that the special vaccine prevents serious complications, if not the disease itself. This vaccine is supplied by the Health Department to Councils, to which application should be made for inoculation.

Disinfection of the nose and mouth. —

Douche — A flat teaspoon full of salt, baking soda, and boric acid dissolved in a quart of warm water.

Sprays — Permanganate of potash, 1 in 1500, or 2% solution of hydrogen peroxide. These may also be used as mouth washes.

Inhalant — Eucalyptus oil, 7 parts; terebene, 2 parts; and menthol, 1 part.

The above have been found satisfactory, but many others are available. Medical advice should be sought as to what is best to use under the circumstances.

Legal obligations. —

(1) Every householder shall immediately send a report, in writing, to the Council of every case of influenza, or any illness resembling influenza, which occurs in the house, and such report shall include the name, age, and sex of the patient, and the exact location of the house.

(2) Every person who suffers from symptoms of influenza shall immediately inform the occupier of the house wherein he resides of his condition.

(3) Every person who has been in contact with a case of influenza shall immediately send a report to the Council, and such report shall include such person's name and address.

(4) No contact and no person suffering from symptoms of influenza shall enter any public building or place where persons are congregated.

(5) Any person who fails to comply with the foregoing regulations, or is guilty of any neglect or disobedience thereof, is liable to a penalty of £20.

By order,
T. W. H. HOLMES,
Secretary.

29

JOURNAL OF THE AMERICAN MEDICAL ASSOCIATION

Failure to Quarantine in Buenos Aires

October 26, 1918

A physician's report from Buenos Aires, Argentina, noted how the failure of authorities to introduce quarantine measures resulted in the rapid spread of influenza throughout the city and then into the countryside.

BUENOS AIRES, OCTOBER 26, 1918. The steamships *Demerara* and the *Infanta Isabel* arrived at Buenos Aires with numerous cases of influenza on board, and there had been several deaths during the voyage. The public health authorities allowed the passengers to disembark without taking any prophylactic measures whatever. Fifteen days later numerous cases of influenza developed in the city, especially in the mail service, in which there were over 100 cases in one day. By another week the infection had spread throughout the entire city thence to numerous points in the interior of the country. It is estimated that there have been 250,000 cases in Buenos Aires alone. Fortunately the disease has been of a mild type, no deaths occurring except nine fatal cases in the Hospital Muñiz. Quite recently the mortality has increased a little, but it is still low. . . . In the majority of the cases improvement is evident by the second to the fifth day, but pronounced depression and anorexia are left. The graver cases developed pulmonary or gastro-intestinal symptoms. Almost all the fatalities were from pneumonia or broncho-pneumonia. . . .

The indecision of the public health authorities has been the object of much criticism. The Departamento Nacional de Higiene has been without a head for several months.

"Buenos Aires Letter," *Journal of the American Medical Association* 71, no. 24 (1918): 2009.

30

E. HENRY CUMMINGS

An Appeal by the Mayor of Freetown, Sierra Leone

September 7, 1918

The Mayor of Freetown, Sierra Leone, a British colony in West Africa, issued an appeal to the general public for help in treating the many who had fallen ill.

I am informed that the Colonial Government have utilised the Model School as a hospital for the accommodation of Influenza patients from among the labouring classes in Freetown.

To enable the scheme to be carried out Volunteers are asked for to supervise the distribution of food and medicines to the patients and to carry out prophylactic measures within the building.

A number of Government officials have volunteered for this work and a commencement has already been made. The assistance so rendered is not sufficient however to adequately deal with the present situation and I earnestly appeal to each and every citizen of Freetown to come forward and aid this movement, either by volunteering for nursing duty at the Model School and at such other temporary hospitals as it may be found necessary to open, or to assist as house to house visitors for the purpose of collecting and removing to the temporary hospitals those of the sick who have no one to look after them, and for whom such attention as will be afforded in the temporary hospital is essential. . . .

I earnestly hope that in a crisis like the present this appeal to the citizens of Freetown will not be in vain.

"The Influenza Epidemic: An Appeal by the Mayor of the City," *Sierra Leone Weekly News*, September 7, 1918, 8.

31

E. EVELYN

A Defense of the Colonial Government's Response to the Flu in Sierra Leone

September 25, 1918

In response to criticism of the way British colonial authorities had handled the deadly pandemic (see Document 57), the Acting Colonial Secretary of Sierra Leone issued a letter defending the actions of his government.

The recent epidemic of influenza has given rise to a number of rumours. It is alleged, for instance, that the disease was introduced through the neglect of the civil authorities in connection with a certain infected ship, that the measures taken to combat it were inadequate and that the European officials showed a culpable indifference to the scourge that was affecting the people. The epidemic will be the subject of a full report in due course; this communiqué will deal only with the reports which have been spread upon the subject.

The infected ship in question was one of His Majesty's Ships and was not under the control, sanitary or otherwise, of the civil authorities. It is not the practice to report the arrival or sanitary state of such ships to the Governor. In the case of this particular ship no such report was made, but within a few hours of her arrival the Governor was informed in conversation with the principal naval authorities that she was infected, that every precaution was being taken, and that no communication was being permitted between the ship and the shore. At the request of the Civil Sanitary authority the ship was moved to a more distant anchorage. The naval authorities consider that the precautions taken were adequate and that the introduction of the epidemic into Freetown was probably due to some other vessel.

As soon as there was reason to suspect the outbreak of epidemic influenza in Freetown orders were issued that new dispensaries should

E. Evelyn, "Communiqué," *Sierra Leone Weekly News,* September 28, 1918, 5.

be opened and that the public should be warned by notices and otherwise of the danger, of the need for precautions, and of the measures taken for providing medicines and disinfectants. The orders were carried out at once. The epidemic spread, however, with unprecedented rapidity[,] prostrating the bulk of the medical staff and most of the population of the town. The Government then opened the Model School as a hospital to feed and care for such patients as could not be attended to adequately by their own friends and families. The nursing staff of this hospital was made up mainly of European officials who had escaped or recovered from the epidemic.

Very little help was given by the general public. An appeal by the Mayor led to one volunteer coming forward with real help. On the other hand there was much criticism by non-helpers and suggestions were made to the Governor and Acting Colonial Secretary and passed on by them to the Principal Medical Officer and Senior Sanitary Officer for their consideration. The Principal Medical Officer was also authorised to engage the services of any local medical men whom he might need for the purpose of strengthening his staff, and any recommendations made by him in this direction were approved at once.

Owing to the importance of medical service at such a time several Government Medical Officers at great personal risk carried on their duties while themselves suffering from the disease. All the medical staff, doctors and nurses, worked with great devotion.

Fourteen European officers volunteered for work in connection with the epidemic, thirteen of them working in relays day and night in attendance on the pauper sick at the Model School. One Government clerk, and one Messenger and one Creole unofficial [*sic*], Mr. Lisk, did similar excellent service. It is to be regretted that their example was not followed more extensively.

Five European Ladies and gentlemen of the unofficial community also assisted the Military in the measures taken by them for nursing or otherwise attending to the victims of the epidemic.

32

OAKLAND, CALIFORNIA, HEALTH DEPARTMENT

Influenza! How to Avoid It! How to Care for Those Who Have It!

1918

In the absence of any effective treatments, local and national governments could do little more than issue directives. In Oakland, California, the local health department advised patients who could not access medical attention to undertake certain measures, and provided specific suggestions as to how to keep the disease from spreading.

The following suggestions of the California State Board of Health may prove of immeasurable value to any man or woman who will read, remember and act upon them in the present great emergency. The counsel here set forth has been prepared after consultation with some of the ablest medical men in America. If you will follow the dictates of this official bulletin, you will be doing your duty to your fellow man and to yourself.

What to Do until the Doctor Comes!

If you feel a sudden chill, followed by muscular pain, headache, backache, unusual tiredness and fever, go to bed at once.

See that there is enough bed clothing to keep you warm.

Open all the windows in your bedroom and keep them open at all times, except in rainy weather.

Take medicine to open the bowels freely.

Take some nourishing food, such as milk, egg-and-milk, or broth every four hours.

Stay in bed until a physician tells you that it is safe to get up.

Allow no one else to sleep in the same room.

"Influenza Advice from the Oakland, California Health Department" (1918). From Vault B 168, California Historical Society, San Francisco.

Protect others by sneezing and coughing into handkerchiefs or cloths, which should be boiled or burned.

Insist that whoever gives you water or food or enters the room for any other purpose shall wear a gauze mask, which may be obtained from the Red Cross or may be made at home of four to six squares of gauze and which should cover the nose and mouth and be tied behind the head.

Remember that these masks must be kept clean, must be put on outside the sick room, must not be handled after they are tied on, and must be boiled five minutes and thoroughly dried every time they are taken off.

TO HOUSEHOLDERS

Keep out of the sick room unless attendance is necessary.

Do not handle articles coming from the sick room until they are boiled.

Allow no visitors, and do not go visiting.

Call a doctor for all inmates who show signs of beginning sickness.

The usual symptoms are: Inflamed and watery eyes, discharging nose, backache, headache, muscular pain, and fever.

Keep away from crowded places, such as "movies," theaters, street cars.

See to it that your children are kept warm and dry, both night and day.

Have sufficient fire in your home to disperse the dampness.

Open your windows at night. If cool weather prevails, add extra bed clothing.

TO WORKERS

Walk to work if possible.

Avoid the person who coughs or sneezes.

Wash your hands before eating.

Make full use of all available sunshine.

Do not use a common towel. It spreads disease.

Should you cough or sneeze, cover nose and mouth with a handkerchief.

Keep out of crowded places. Walk in the open air rather than go to crowded places of amusement.

Sleep is necessary for well-being — avoid overexertion. Eat good clean food.

Keep away from houses where there are cases of influenza.

If sick, no matter how slightly, see a physician.

If you have had influenza, stay in bed until your doctor says you can safely get up.

TO NURSES

Keep clean. Isolate your patients.

When in attendance upon patients, wear a mask which will cover both the nose and the mouth. When the mask is once in place, do not handle it.

Change the mask every two hours. Owing to the scarcity of gauze, boil for five minutes and rinse, then use the gauze again.

Wash your hands each time you come in contact with the patient. Use bichloride of mercury, 1–1000, or Liquor Cresol compound, 1–100, for hand disinfection.

Obtain at least seven hours' sleep each twenty-four hours. Eat plenty of good, clean food.

Walk in the fresh air daily.

Sleep with your windows open.

Insist that the patient cough, sneeze, or expectorate into cloths that may be disinfected or burned.

Boil all dishes.

Keep patients warm.

33

UNITED STATES PUBLIC HEALTH SERVICE

Warning Notice about Influenza

1918

Although there was no known treatment for the flu, authorities did provide appropriate recommendations for preventing transmission of the disease. Here, a notice from the United States Public Health Service explains how the disease is spread, and advises Americans to avoid crowds and contact.

Treasury Department, United States Public Health Service influenza advice, 1918. From Library of Congress, Rare Book and Special Collections Division. Library of Congress, American Memory, http://memory.loc/gov/ammem.

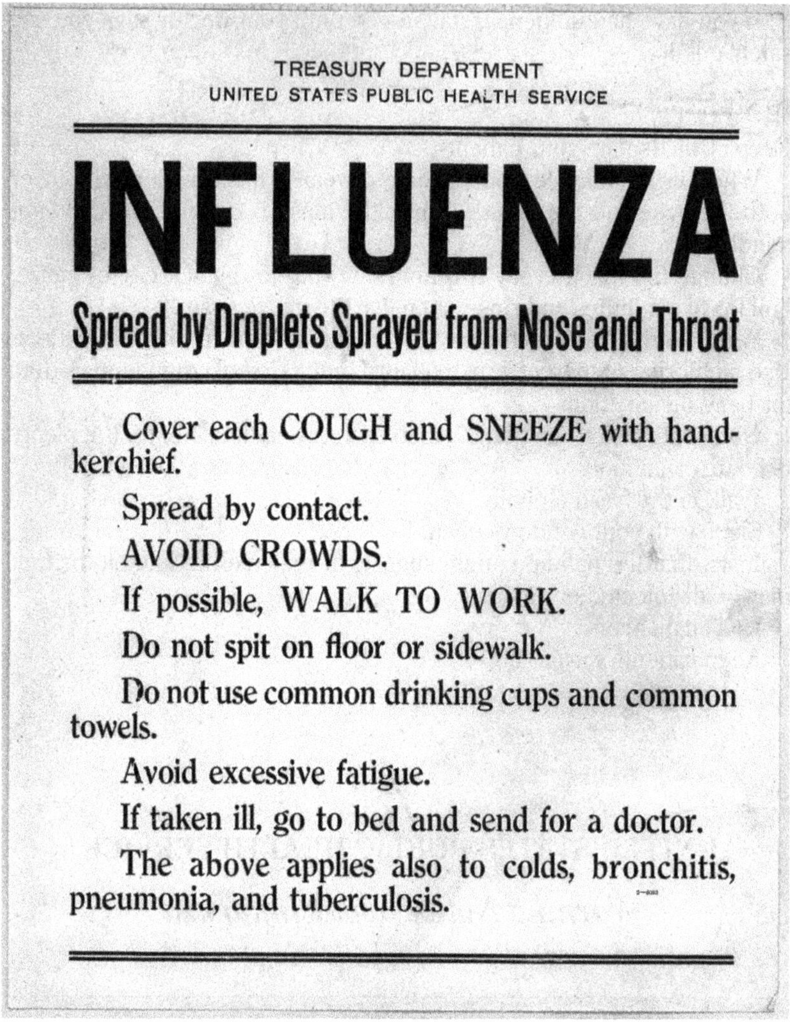

TREASURY DEPARTMENT

UNITED STATES PUBLIC HEALTH SERVICE

INFLUENZA

Spread by Droplets Sprayed from Nose and Throat

Cover each COUGH and SNEEZE with handkerchief.

Spread by contact.

AVOID CROWDS.

If possible, WALK TO WORK.

Do not spit on floor or sidewalk.

Do not use common drinking cups and common towels.

Avoid excessive fatigue.

If taken ill, go to bed and send for a doctor.

The above applies also to colds, bronchitis, pneumonia, and tuberculosis.

34

NORTH CAROLINA STATE BOARD OF HEALTH

The Way the Germans Did It at Chateau-Thierry; The Way North Carolinians Do It at Home

October 1919

North Carolina authorities urged preventive measures such as wearing masks and covering one's mouth when coughing or sneezing by comparing the effects of the flu on the population to the murderous assaults of the German army on the battlefield.

North Carolina State Board of Health, *The Health Bulletin* XXXIV, no. 10, October 1919.

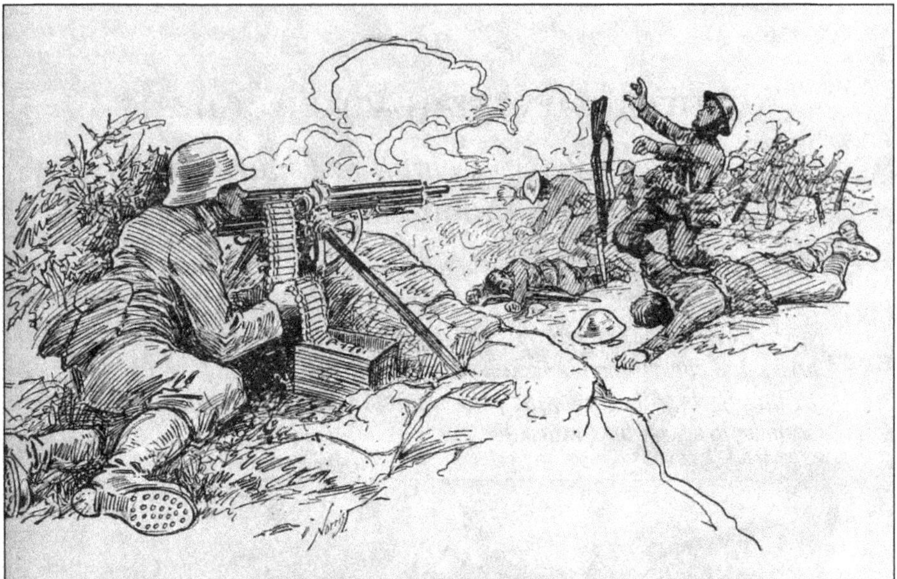

THE WAY THE GERMANS DID IT AT CHATEAU-THIERRY

During the recent war approximately 1000 men from North Carolina were killed in battle.

THE WAY NORTH CAROLINIANS DO IT AT HOME

During the epidemic last fall and winter 13,644 North Carolinians laid down their lives to a "spit-borne" disease—influenza !

35

GOVERNMENT OF NEW SOUTH WALES

Proclamation

February 3, 1919

As the pandemic spread, the Government of New South Wales went as far as prohibiting certain public gatherings, including church services, and closing public spaces from billiard halls to library reading rooms.

To the People of New South Wales

A danger greater than war faces the State of New South Wales and threatens the lives of all. Each day the progress of the battle is published in the Press. Watch out for it. Follow the advice given and the fight can be won.

Already the efforts made by the Government have had the effect of keeping the New South Wales figures down. But everybody is not yet working, so from TO-DAY on the Government insists that the many shall not be placed in danger for the few and that

EVERYONE SHALL WEAR A MASK

Those who are not doing so are not showing their independence — they are only showing their indifference for the lives of others — for the lives of the women and the helpless little children who cannot help themselves.

Cabinet Decisions:
At a special meeting of the cabinet, held yesterday, the following recommendations . . . were adopted —

Proclamation of the N.S.W. Government regulations to control the epidemic. From the *Sydney Morning Herald*, February 3, 1919.

1. Long-Distance Trains. — No need to restrict railway travel in New South Wales as yet, although it may be necessary to do so at any moment.
2. Hotel Bars, Restaurants, Tea Houses. — Not to be closed at the present time, but the 250 cubic feet restrictions to apply to them.
3. Retail Shops. — Space regulations to apply: also, prohibition of Bargain and Changing tables, and a recommendation that orders be telephoned.
4. Church Services. — Prohibition of both indoor and outdoor services.
5. Auction Rooms. — Prohibition of all sales in rooms.
6. Libraries. — Reading rooms to be closed down.
7. Billiard Rooms. — To be closed.
8. Race Meetings. — Prohibited.
9. Theatres, Music Halls, Indoor Public Entertainments. — Prohibited.
10. Beaches. — No restrictions to be placed upon the free use of the beaches on the grounds that the risk of infection is likely to be more than counterbalanced by the benefits that will ensue.
11. Open Air Meetings in the Domain and Other Places. — Prohibited.
12. Churches and Schools Outside the County of Cumberland. — Not to be closed. Local authorities not to act on own initiative but to be asked to refer to the Public Health Department in every instance.

GENERAL RECOMMENDATION.

That, as far as possible, the people be encouraged during the course of the epidemic [to take] all possible advantage of fresh air as a means of increasing both the natural resistance to infection, and of lessening the risk of infection, and also to avoid crowds.

W. A. Holman, Premier.

36

DAILY EXPRESS (LONDON)

Quinine and Cinnamon to the Rescue

June 22, 1918

The pandemic of 1918 confronted physicians with the near-intolerable fact that they had no idea how to treat the disease. Unable to provide effective treatment or to prevent further outbreaks, doctors tried a range of treatments to defeat influenza, only to fall short. In this news item from June 1918, a London physician describes what we might regard as folk remedies.

A previous visitation of influenza earned for itself the significant appellation of "La Grippe." The present epidemic in London is popularly known as "Spanish Flu," due to a connection, real or imaginary, with the "mysterious malady" which raged in Madrid a few weeks ago.

It is clear that the malady is not confined to Army camps. Many banks, business houses, and the like are having to carry on with sadly depleted staffs owing to the ravages of the disease. The medical officer for Westminster told a "Daily Express" representative yesterday that no one was immune.

"People who are run down fall easier victims than those in a robust state of health," he said. "The best way to ward off the illness is to take plenty of fresh air and avoid overcrowded places. That, of course, is very difficult in these days, when we all have to take a turn at straphanging in the tubes and every railway train is overcrowded.

"It has been found that a small dose of quinine is a good preventive. Some people pin their faith to formamint [see Document 38] and cinnamon tablets. Cinnamon, as a matter of fact, is a valuable specific as a preventive in the case of epidemics such as this.

"The present form of influenza seldom lasts much more than a week. Some people are up and about again in four days. There is only one way of dealing with it when you are attacked—go straight to bed. The symptoms are unmistakable."

"Quinine and Cinnamon to the Rescue," *Daily Express* (London), June 22, 1918, 3.

37

Z. DIONYSIUS LEOMY

Letter to the Editor of the Sierra Leone Weekly News

September 14, 1918

One lay reader of the Sierra Leone Weekly News *offered his suggestions for treatment. They do not appear to differ very much in kind from those of medical personnel.*

Sir,—Kindly publish for the information of the sufferers from Influenza, the preventative and cure; many have tried it and are now quite well.

(i). Boil teabush, beat (pulverise) a little ginger and add to the teabush; strain, and drink when warm. This should be used early in the morning, and at night.

(ii). Put a piece of Camphor in a tumbler, full of COLD water, drink this three or four times a day, keeping the tumbler always full.

Use purgatives occasionally, keep the house ventilated and avoid extremes of temperature.

Z. Dionysius Leomy, "The Influenza Epidemic," *Sierra Leone Weekly News,* September 14, 1918, 1.

38

"Why Catch Their Influenza?"

1919

Companies took advantage of the flu to hawk their wares, tailoring their ad campaigns to address ways to prevent or treat the disease. Here, a British advertisement for Formamint, "The Germ Killing Throat Tablet," suggests that the throat lozenge can prevent influenza.

Advertisement, Formamint, 1919.

Why catch their Influenza?
YOU need not! Just carry Formamint with you and suck these delicious tablets whenever you are in danger of being infected by other people.
"Suck at least four or five a day"—so says Dr. Hopkirk in his standard work "Influenza"—for "in Formamint we possess the best means of preventing the infective processes which, if neglected, may lead to serious complications."
Seeing that such complications often lead to Pneumonia, Bronchitis, and other dangerous diseases, it is surely worth while to protect yourself by this safe, certain, and inexpensive means. Protect the children, too, for their delicate little organisms are very exposed to germ-attack, especially during school-epidemics. Be careful, however, not to confuse Formamint with so-called formalin tablets, but see that it bears the name of the sole manufacturers: Genatosan, Limited (British Purchasers of Sanatogen Co.), 12, Chenies Street, London, W.C. 1. (Chairman: The Viscountess Rhondda.)
"Attack the germs before they attack you!"
Though genuine Formamint is scarce your chemist can still obtain it for you at the pre-war price—2/2 per bottle. Order it to-day.
Formamint
THE GERM KILLING THROAT TABLET

39

THE DAILY HERALD (LONDON)

On Behalf of the Invalids

December 21, 1918

Apothecaries in England couldn't keep pace with the demand for patent medicines thought to be effective remedies.

It is deeply to be regretted that the influenza epidemic coincided with a shortage of Bovril.

On behalf of the invalids, Bovril Ltd. wish to thank all those who refrain from buying Bovril during this period. The unselfish action of those consumers allows the available supplies to go to those who stand in greater need of Bovril.

More bottles and therefore more Bovril will be available early in the New Year.

Advertisement, *The Daily Herald* (London), December 21, 1918.

40

BRITISH MEDICAL JOURNAL

Influenza and the Shortage of Doctors

November 2, 1918

The presence of so massive a pandemic in the midst of the greatest war ever fought to date meant that medical care on the home front often proved unavailable. With so many physicians, nurses, and orderlies serving in the armed forces of the various belligerent countries, civilian populations often went unattended by medical professionals; conversely,

---

"Influenza and the Shortage of Doctors," *British Medical Journal*, November 2, 1919, 495–96.

the demand for medical personnel in the home countries put pressure on the medical resources available at the front.

The Central Medical War Committee is taking all steps in its power to meet the situation created by the epidemic of influenza, for the calls arising from it have greatly aggravated the shortage of civilian practitioners. . . . Owing to the prevalence of influenza for some months past the calls on the civil medical profession had been heavy, and, simultaneously, severe fighting on a great scale on all the fronts had imposed additional strain on our medical resources. Concurrently with the increasing spread of influenza the number of doctors employed on medical boards had been reduced, and in order to further reinforce the doctors available for the civil population, medical examinations of recruits in advance had been suspended for the present, while the medical staffs of hospitals had been strengthened so far as resources permit. [Director of National Service] Sir Auckland Geddes expressed his deep appreciation of the way in which the medical profession has co-operated with the Ministry in meeting unprecedented and often conflicting demands for medical personnel. He explained that, owing to the heavy casualties among R.A.M.C. [Royal Army Medical Corps] officers, there is now a great demand for young fit doctors for the fighting line.

41

MATEO ARRIOLA MORENO

Influenza in Paraguay

1918

Chief of Clinical Medical Services at the National Hospital of Asuncion in Paraguay, Dr. Mateo Arriola Moreno treated between eighty and one hundred patients in fifteen days, during an intense outbreak of influenza in Asuncion, Paraguay. As his essay for the medical journal La semana médica (The Week in Medicine) *indicates, he employed treatments that*

Mateo Arriola Moreno, "Influenza in Paraguay," *La semana médica* (*The Week in Medicine*) 25 (1918): 785–86. Translated by Mary K. Long.

many doctors throughout the Western world utilized. They included a bewildering array of medicines, minerals, serums, and herbs.

In all of these cases of influenza, I have successfully used quinine salts, at a small dose, especially quinine valerianate 0.25 to 0.30 centigrams, mixed [into wafers] with pyramidon 0.15 centigrams and caffeine citrate 0.10 centigrams.

I have administered from two to three wafers a day and on occasion just one wafer, depending on whether or not the patient had a high fever or if the fever had disappeared, in which case I stopped the dosage immediately.

I have visited my patients on a daily basis and none has complained of ringing in the ears, deafness, etc., on the contrary they told me that the wafers had an admirable effect on the fever and pains that they suffered from. I have used it on my own person with the same success.

So, I want to believe that febrifuges [drugs used to decrease fever] used in the proper dose and at the right time, calm the fever and the pains that are so bothersome for the poor patients who suffer from influenza.

Furthermore, for coughs which are so persistent in these patients, I have used codeine, opium, belladonna, dionina, etc.

In pneumonia cases, I have successfully used *neumo-Méndez* [an antiviral vaccine] in patients who presented with their organs in good enough condition to fight the illness. In addition to this medicine, [I have used] common cupping glasses, oxygen, baths and mustard plasters, bloodletting, and above all, heart care, with the common tonics. Regardless of their condition, I have given all my influenza patients some of the following tonics: *digalena* and *estrofanto*, especially mixed with expectorant drinks, and I have not been sorry, except in one fatal case (of double pneumonia), all the rest having recuperated, possibly because they were good cases.

In addition I have frequently observed patients with abundant nose bleeds (epistaxis). In another case, to which I was called as an emergency, I observed multiple hemorrhages: from the nose, from the mouth, the tongue had such a large clot that it covered the whole tongue and impeded the administration of medicine and food; in addition, other bleeding presented include enerorrhagia [anal bleeding] and metrorrhagia [bleeding from the vagina, unrelated to menstruation] as well as exanthema [rash caused by fever] all over the body, concentrations of hemorrhagic spots.

In these cases I have successfully used adrenaline with a saline solution, ergot, horse serum and *Wité* peptone from the Argentine Biological Institute.

I want to finish now by leaving out some cases so as not to go on too long. And so I will say that from the point of view of the circulatory system I have in almost all cases observed a reduction in the number of pulsations (bradycardia) from 85 to 95 (sic) with a relatively high temperature 39 and 39.6 degrees Celsius, [102.2–103.28° F], tense pulse.

In conclusion, then, influenza has presented in our region in two forms: mild and serious, in some cases even sudden and devastating. But the majority were mild, especially in subjects who presented with healthy organs: heart, kidney, liver and who did not do anything reckless. In these cases the daily visit and attention from the doctor is very effective.

Serious cases presented in subjects already at the age of arteriosclerosis, alcoholic, with cardiac problems, nephritic [with kidney problems] or with liver problems or in young subjects from 20–35 years old, who appeared to be relatively healthy, but who have weakened some of their major organs: heart, liver, due to the special idiosyncrasy of each subject and subjects belonging to the same family.

42

SOUTH AFRICAN MEDICAL RECORD

Notes on the Influenza Epidemic

December 14, 1918

Physicians prescribed a number of often-contradictory treatments, as the reports by three South African doctors demonstrate. All three were printed in the same issue of the South African Medical Record.

"Notes on the Influenza Epidemic," *South African Medical Record*, December 14, 1918, 363–65.

Dr. R. Broom, Herbert and Hay Districts
When the epidemic started, I succeeded in getting a small supply of catarrhal vaccine from the Clinsearch Laboratory, and I always had a fair supply of pneumococcus vaccine (Clinsearch), and though the supply for some time was lamentably short, I was able to control my worst cases from the beginning. Later on we had an unlimited supply of Lister vaccine, and started prophylactic inoculations on a large scale. The results have been eminently satisfactory.

Out of many hundreds of whites and natives inoculated I am not aware of any deaths in the Herbert district, or of any cases of pneumonia. . . .

I took the liberty of giving advice to all quite contrary to that sent by the Government on circulars. Especially, I let it be known that, in my opinion, aspirin was a most dangerous drug, which ought, in influenza cases, on no account to be used. I also advised that brandy be strictly avoided, and in no case gave quinine.

Dr. E. E. Wood, Tokai Convict Prison and Porter Reformatory
One of the most distressing conditions in respect to the recent visit of epidemic influenza to South Africa was the extreme uncertainty which existed in medical minds as to the best method of dealing with the outbreak. We had a rough idea that care was necessary, that fresh air was an essential, but as to medical treatment our minds were fogged. Aspirin was advised and even advertised in the public press, very injudiciously I think, and probably the indiscriminate use of aspirin was responsible for a number of deaths.

. . . The treatment which was carried out in routine, modified as necessary for severe or atypical cases, was as follows:—

On admission each patient was given a good dose of hot sulphate of magnesia, followed by sod. salicyl. grains 15 and tr. digitalis minims 5 every four hours. This continued until bronchial symptoms appeared, when pot. iodid. grains 7½ and ammon. carb. grains 3 were given every four hours.

Dr. R. Leigh, Reitz, O.F.S.
My experience of the treatment of influenza is mainly negative. The only things of undoubted value are care of patients, going to bed in good time, and not getting up until convalescence is assured. All treatment appears to fail in severe cases, especially when the lungs are affected.

So far as I have observed, inoculation, preventive or for treatment, is of doubtful value.

The chief drugs I have found of value are caffeine, digitalis with strychnia, and, perhaps, ipecacuanha.

Stimulants are also of much use.

But, in severe cases, all things fail. The great trouble seems to be, not the severity of the pneumonia or other affection of the lungs, but the direct depressing effect of the influenza poison.

43

INDIAN MEDICAL GAZETTE

A Criticism of Indian Physicians

February 1919

The Indian Medical Gazette, *serving the Anglo-Indian medical community and its patients, published an article disdainful of the efforts of Indian physicians and medical practitioners to address the flu. But remedies resorted to by indigenous physicians trained in Western methods differed little from those of their colonial counterparts. The attitude of the writer reflects a distinct unease among Britons at the prospect of Indians "mimicking" their colonial overlords.*

We have been deluged with letters (too often almost illegible and written on scraps of paper) on the subject of the treatment of cases of influenza or "war fever" as some of our correspondents childishly call it following irresponsible writers in the daily press.

If we are to judge by our correspondence there are many "specifics." A well-known medical officer pins his faith on laudanum (5m.), tincture of belladonna (5m.) with camphor water—. . . it must be taken at the onset of the attack—when by-the-bye it is not at hand. Another writes of the value of chlorate of potash and quinine, and adds that digitalis is "to be given in cases having a weak heart."

Another writer swears by iodine, one-drop doses of the *tinctura iodi fortis* with one drop of chloroform. If pneumonia has set in he prescribes

"Treatment of Influenza," *Indian Medical Gazette*, February 1919, 68.

camphor, ipecac., creosote and several other drugs in one fell mixture. For "home treatment" the same writer prescribes ginger, jaggery [concentrated cane sugar], betel-nut, black pepper, "in every stage of the disease." The only wise remark in his letter is on the necessity of good ventilation. . . .

All this goes merely to prove that there is no specific for the disease, —early rest in bed and treatment of symptoms is what is needed; but it also shows the profound belief of Indian practitioners in drugs.

44

CHINA MEDICAL JOURNAL

A Criticism of Chinese Treatment of Influenza

January 1919

The China Medical Journal, *the organ of the Medical Missionary Association of China, which largely comprised British and American Protestants seeking to establish Western medicine in China, regularly lampooned the practices used by traditional Chinese physicians. The satire below makes traditional medicine look ridiculous, although recent scientists have argued that traditional Chinese medicine may well have acted to reduce the severity of flu symptoms in China.*

The temples are well massaged, then the nose is worked backwards and forward for a time, next the lobe of each ear is drawn down to its full limit a number of times. The nape of the neck is well curried with an inverted bowl, then the small of the back is done, also the cavity at the back of the knee, and last of all on each side of the shin bone. Those who receive this treatment are said to recover very quickly.

"Chinese Treatment of Influenza," *China Medical Journal*, January 1919, 98.

45

BEULAH GRIBBLE

Influenza in a Kentucky Coal-Mining Camp

1919

In the absence of effective medical care, nursing offered patients the best treatment they were likely to receive. Registered nurse Beulah Gribble traveled by train from Chicago to care for influenza patients at a coal-mining camp in Kentucky at the height of the second wave in October 1918. She paints a picture of a neat and well-run camp, quite different from the logging camp described in Document 8, although the incidence of suffering seems not to have been any less as a result.

This is a coal-mining camp in southeast Kentucky, and is beautifully located among the mountains. A branch of the Cumberland River flows through the valley and the little cottages are built on the narrow level strip of land along the river, and up the mountain sides. These cottages are of four rooms and are very comfortable, —having good light and ventilation. . . . There are 2,500 inhabitants and up to the time the epidemic came, they had been in good health.

We found that the two doctors had been confined to their homes on account of the influenza for several days; they were just returning to their work. Miss F., the nurse, had been doing the doctoring and nursing, working day and night. We could not say enough for one who had worked so faithfully under such discouraging conditions, and although at the time we arrived she was tired and over-worked, she had not thought of giving up. The estimated number of sick was 600. . . .

We met that afternoon and divided the camp into three parts, each nurse taking a part. We carried medicines and gave them to the patients as the doctors had instructed us, for it was impossible for them to call at all the homes, so it became necessary to do more than nursing. We gave nursing care as far as possible, and to others we gave medicine and

---

Beulah Gribble, RN, "Experiences during the Epidemic, III: Influenza in a Kentucky Coal-Mining Camp," *American Journal of Nursing* 19, no. 8 (1919): 609–11.

instruction. Our medicines were aspirin, calomel, and castor oil, C. C. pills, or other cathartics.

I called the first afternoon at twelve homes and found from one to six patients in each, all very sick. Their temperatures were as high as 105 degrees in many cases. Conditions were distressing, due not only to the sickness, but to the fact that the doctors could not get to all to give them medical attention. Neighbors helped each other in giving food and general care wherever possible, and in several homes where there was no one to assist, Miss S., the "Y" secretary, sent soup which was made at the "Y" building. . . .

Some of the people lived in queer, out-of-the-way places and it was impossible to see them as often as necessary, and in families where every member was sick and there was no one to do anything, other means had to be employed. Therefore, we decided to turn the "Y" building into a hospital, and move the sickest patients there. This building was a most acceptable hospital, having a large entrance hall with a large room on either side. In one room we had the women and children and in the other the men. There was also a room upstairs where we put convalescent patients. . . .

Seventeen patients were brought in on Sunday afternoon, October 27. As there was no ambulance department in the camp, the men went out with stretchers and brought in the patients. In one instance we took in a whole family, father, mother and six children. When I left all had recovered except the two babies, who were slowly improving. Before starting the hospital, there had been only two deaths, a baby and a colored man. Everyone in the camp assisted in preparing the building for a hospital. The men cleared out the rooms, scrubbed floors, then brought in the cots, while the teachers cleaned and scrubbed the kitchen and toilet rooms. While they were doing this, the women in their homes were making sheets, gowns, and numerous other necessary things. Everyone was busy helping. . . .

We could only estimate the exact number of patients, but there were at least a thousand, with only twelve deaths. The people, with the exception of a few, were English-speaking, very pleasant, kind, and appreciative of our efforts. After about eighteen days, conditions had greatly improved, the sick were better, and few new cases developed, so Miss M. and I were dismissed from the nursing force.

The work was hard and depressing, but well worth while. We slept at the town's one hotel, a clean, well kept inn that served excellent food. Every one in town was good to us and eager to help, and after the worst was over, we were glad to have had our share in it.

46

M. K. B.

A Two Weeks' Assignment

1919

A Florida nurse identified only by her initials, M. K. B. was a member of the Red Cross when the influenza epidemic broke out. She asked the Southern Division headquarters of the Red Cross to give her an assignment and was sent to North Carolina, reporting to the secretary of the State Board of Health. Her reminiscences reflect both the heartbreak and the sense of accomplishment that nursing brought her.

From Raleigh, Dr. Rankin sent me to Morehead City, a village of about three thousand inhabitants, situated on Bogue Sound and the Atlantic Ocean. About two-thirds of the inhabitants are fishermen and their very large families. . . .

In one room [of a cottage she attended] lay a woman, the dirtiest white human being that I have ever seen. The husband seemed to feel very little responsibility, although he worked regularly and made $5.00 a day. A daughter, by a former marriage, lay in a room across the hall, with her ill husband, the two being on a single bed. A son ill with influenza and having an attack of gall stone colic was in another room. With a generous supply of hot water and soap, borrowed from a neighbor, we spent almost the entire afternoon in cleaning the cottage and the people. The beds were bare of sheets and pillow cases, but some new cotton blankets and bed linen were procured for each of the beds. . . . I felt more than repaid for my efforts by the expression on the face of the little two-year-old baby girl, after I had bathed her and dressed her in clean fresh clothes. Her little head was covered with vermin and her dear little body was emaciated for lack of proper food, but she was the only member of that family that escaped the influenza.

Considering the lack of space, it was remarkable that so few cases of pneumonia developed, for the majority of the cottages had only three

M. K. B., "A Two Weeks' Assignment," *American Journal of Nursing* 19, no. 8 (1919): 607–9.

rooms, a great many of them only two. In one room, the family, consisting usually of from five to eight children and the father and mother would sleep on two beds. The one redeeming feature was the abundance of fresh air, because of the numerous cracks.

47

UNITED STATES NAVY

Awards and Commendations to Medical Staff

1918–1919

A number of medical personnel received the Navy Cross and Letters of Commendation for the service they rendered during the influenza epidemic. Some of them gave their lives in the process.

Personnel Awarded the Navy Cross

Hidell, Marie Louise, Nurse, U.S. Navy.
For distinguished service and devotion to duty while serving at the Naval Hospital, Philadelphia, Pa. During the epidemic of the influenza, worked day and night among the patients until stricken with the disease, as a result of which she lost her life on September 28, 1918.

McGuire, Lee W., Lieutenant Commander, U.S. Navy.
For distinguished service in the line of his profession while serving at the U.S. Naval Hospital, Chelsea, Mass., in developing a convalescent influenza-pneumonia serum, which has proved of very great value in reducing mortality from 38 to 4 per cent, and for general service at the hospital.

Harry R. Stringer, ed., *The Navy Book of Distinguished Service: An Official Compendium of the Names and Citations of the Men of the United States Navy, Marine Corps, Army and Foreign Governments Who Were Decorated by the Navy Department for Extraordinary Gallantry and Conspicuous Service Above and Beyond the Call of Duty in the World War* (Washington, D.C.: Fassett Publishing Company, 1921), 81–209.

Miller, Carey F., Hospital Apprentice First Class, U.S. Navy.
For distinguished service and devotion to duty while serving in the Naval Base Hospital at Hampton Roads. During an epidemic of influenza he worked day and night amongst the patients until stricken with the disease as a result of which he lost his life.

Murphy, Lillian M., Nurse, U.S. Navy.
For distinguished service and devotion to duty while serving at the Naval Base Hospital, Hampton Roads, Va. During the epidemic of influenza, worked day and night among the patients until stricken with the disease, as a result of which she lost her life.

Place, Edna E., Nurse, U.S. Navy.
For distinguished service and devotion to duty, while serving at the Naval Hospital, Philadelphia, Pa. During the epidemic of influenza, worked day and night among the patients until stricken with the disease, as a result of which she lost her life on September 28, 1918.

Poyer, John M., Commander, U.S. Navy.
For exceptionally meritorious service in a duty of great responsibility as governor of American Samoa, for wise and successful administration of his office and especially for the extraordinarily successful measures by which American Samoa was kept absolutely immune from the epidemic of influenza at a time when in the neighboring islands of the Samoan group more than 10,000 deaths occurred, and when the percentage of deaths throughout the Polynesian Islands as a group, is reported to have ranged from 30 to 40 per cent of the population.

Redden, William R., Lieutenant (Medical Corps), U.S. Navy.
For distinguished service in the line of his profession while serving at the United States Naval Hospital, Chelsea, Mass., in developing a convalescent influenza-pneumonia serum, which has proven of very great value in reducing mortality from 38 to 4 per cent, and for general service at the hospital.

US Navy Nurses Receiving a Letter of Commendation for Service during the Influenza of 1918

Brooke, Elsie, Chief Nurse, U.S. Navy.
While Serving as Chief Nurse at the U.S. Naval Hospital, Chelsea, Mass., she exhibited highly commendable devotion to duty in attending to the sick, particularly during the influenza epidemic in the fall of 1918.

Pringle, Martha E., Chief Nurse, U.S. Navy.
As Chief Nurse at the U.S. Naval Hospital, Philadelphia, Pa., and in charge of the nurses of three Civilian Hospitals, she performed arduous, dangerous and efficient service, especially during the epidemic of influenza in September and October, 1918.

4

Consequences and Repercussions of the Pandemic

48

NEW YORK TIMES

2,000 Children Need Care: Measures Taken to Aid Children of Influenza Victims

November 9, 1918

The heavy toll that the influenza epidemic took on the adult population meant that it left scores of orphaned children in its wake in just about every community it struck. Here, the New York Times *reports on the numbers of children in need of temporary or permanent care, as parents succumbed to the disease, while also noting a decrease in the number of new cases and deaths.*

Health Commissioner Royal S. Copeland said yesterday that there were approximately 21,000 children who had been made half or full orphans by the Spanish Influenza epidemic. In 7,200 families either one parent or both had died. Of these families about 700 would need aid from the city, he said, and about 2,000 children would be affected.

In the emergency, Dr. Copeland said, institutions and individuals had offered assistance. In some cases only temporary care would be required until relatives could give proper guardianship. More than fifty persons, he said, had asked to be permitted to adopt a child. Most of the requests were for children 1 to 3 years of age. In every case,

New York Times, November 9, 1918.

Dr. Copeland said, great care was taken in investigating the responsibility of applicants.

Leo Lerner, President of the Hebrew National Orphan House, 52 St. Mark's Place, said yesterday that the house would accept from 75 to 100 orphans. The institution has begun to enlarge its accommodations. The Hebrew Kindergarten and Day Nursery, at 35 Montgomery Street, has opened a special ward, with trained nurses in attendance, for the care of children whose mothers are ill with influenza. The institution has also undertaken the care of children whose mothers have died recently.

Reports yesterday showed a decrease in new cases of influenza. . . .

Yesterday's figures show a decrease of 169 new cases of influenza over the preceding twenty-four hours, a decrease of 30 cases of pneumonia, 49 less pneumonia deaths, and 68 fewer deaths from influenza.

49

MARY McCARTHY

Orphaned by the Flu

1946

American writer Mary McCarthy (1912–1989) provided an account of the flu that killed her parents and left her and her brother Kevin orphaned at a very young age. Some of her memories (such as her father holding a gun on the train conductor to keep him from putting them off the train) proved to be untrue when she tried to corroborate them, but the passage below, however ironically delivered, gives a poignant sense of the loss suffered by so many whose loved ones died in the pandemic.

Poor Roy's children, as commiseration damply styled us, could not afford illusions, in the family opinion. Our father had put us beyond the pale by dying suddenly of influenza and taking our young mother with him, a defection that was remarked on with horror and grief commingled, as though our mother had been a pretty secretary with whom he

From Mary McCarthy, *Memories of a Catholic Girlhood* (New York: Harvest Books, Harcourt, 1993; originally 1946), 29–30, 35–36, 37.

had wantonly absconded into the irresponsible paradise of the hereafter. Our reputation was clouded by this misfortune. . . .

[My grandmother] had accommodated us all during those fatal weeks of the influenza epidemic, when no hospital beds were to be had and people went about with masks or stayed shut up in their houses, and the awful fear of contagion paralyzed all services and made each man an enemy to his neighbor. One by one, we had been carried off the train which had brought us from distant Puget Sound to make a new home in Minneapolis. Waving good-by in the Seattle depot, we had not known that we had carried the flu with us into our drawing rooms, along with the presents and the flowers, but, one after another, we had been struck down as the train proceeded eastward. We children did not understand whether the chattering of our teeth and Mama's lying torpid in the berth were not somehow a part of the trip (until then, serious illness, in our minds, had been associated with innovations—it had always brought home a new baby), and we began to be sure that it was all an adventure when we saw our father draw a revolver on the conductor who was trying to put us off the train at a small wooden station in the middle of the North Dakota prairie. On the platform at Minneapolis, there were stretchers, a wheel chair, redcaps, distraught officials, and, beyond them, in the crowd, my grandfather's rosy face, cigar, and cane, my grandmother's feathered hat, imparting an air of festivity to this strange and confused picture, making us children certain that our illness was the beginning of a delightful holiday.

We awoke to reality in the sewing room several weeks later, to an atmosphere of castor oil, rectal thermometers, cross nurses, and efficiency, and though we were shut out from the knowledge of what had happened so close to us, just out of our hearing—a scandal of the gravest character, a coming and going of priests and undertakers and coffins (Mama and Daddy, they assured us, had gone to get well in the hospital)—we became aware, even as we woke from our fevers, that everything, including ourselves, was different. We had shrunk, as it were, and faded, like the flannel pajamas we wore, which during these few weeks had grown, doubtless from the disinfectant they were washed in, wretchedly thin and shabby. The behavior of the people around us, abrupt, careless, and preoccupied, apprised us without any ceremony of our diminished importance. Our value had paled, and a new image of ourselves—the image, if we had guessed it, of the orphan—was already forming in our minds. We had not known we were spoiled, but now this word, entering our vocabulary for the first time, served to define the change for us and to herald the new order. Before we got sick, we were spoiled; that was what was the matter now, and everything we could not understand, everything unfamiliar and displeasing, took on a certain plausibility when related to this fresh concept. . . .

The happy life we had had . . . was a poor preparation, in truth, for the future that now opened up to us. Our new instructors could hardly be blamed for a certain impatience with our parents, who had been so lacking in foresight. It was to everyone's interest, decidedly, that we should forget the past—the quicker, the better—and a steady disparagement of our habits . . . prepared us to accept a loss that was, in any case, irreparable. Like all children, we wished to conform, and the notion that our former ways had been somehow ridiculous and unsuitable made the memory of them falter a little, like a child's recitation to strangers. We no longer demanded our due, and the wish to see our parents insensibly weakened. Soon we ceased to speak of it, and thus, without tears or tantrums, we came to know they were dead.

50

ERICH VON LUDENDORFF

The Offensive in the West

1919

General Erich von Ludendorff (1865–1937) headed the war effort in Germany. In spring 1918, the Germans embarked upon what they regarded as their last opportunity to break the stalemate between the armies of the Allies and the Central Powers on the western front. At first, their efforts proved effective, enabling the German army to advance to within firing range of Paris. But by late June, the German offensive had stalled, in part, Ludendorff insisted, as a result of his troops being laid low by influenza. On July 15, German forces attacked again, hoping for one final breakthrough that might afford them victory. But the French and the Americans held fast, and then the French counterattacked on July 18, driving back the German army at what became known as the Second Battle of the Marne. This loss proved to be the end of Germany's ability to mount further offensives; all it could do now was to retreat and hold on long enough to seek a peace that wouldn't cripple the nation.

Erich von Ludendorff, *Ludendorff's Own Story: August 1914–November 1918* (New York: Harper & Brothers, 1919), II:252, 277, 316–17.

The men's rations were sufficient, but very inferior to those of the enemy. . . . Health had so far been good. The first cases of influenza appeared, but the medical officers classified them as slight.

[*Within weeks, conditions had changed dramatically.*] . . . Our army had suffered. Influenza was rampant, and the army group of Crown Prince Rupprecht was particularly afflicted. It was a grievous business having to listen every morning to the chiefs of staffs' recital of the number of influenza cases, and their complaints about the weakness of their troops if the English attacked again. However, the English were not ready yet. The number of influenza cases diminished, although it often left a greater weakness in its wake than the doctors realized.

. . . I inquired into the reasons for our failure of the 18th [July]. The men no longer believed in the possibility of an attack [by the Allies] . . . . The rapid movement of the numerous fast tanks in the high corn increased the effect of the surprise. To all this must be added the diminished strength of the divisions, the result partly of influenza and partly of the monotonous diet.

51

GERMAN OFFICE OF SANITATION

Influenza Mortality, German Armed Forces

1917–1919

Although reports of influenza were not made public in Germany during the war, German authorities attempted to keep track of deaths due to the disease in the armed forces. The graph and figures published by Sanitätsbericht über das deutsche heer im Weltkriege 1914/1918 *[Bureau of Sanitation] appeared in 1934. In contrast to the patterns for the United States and for other European countries, influenza appears to have killed a great many German soldiers in June and July of 1918, during the first wave of the disease.*

Sanitätsbericht über das deutsche heer im Weltkriege 1914/1918, Vol. 3 (Mittler & Sohn, 1934). From Andrew Price-Smith, *Contagion and Chaos: Disease, Ecology, and National Security in the Era of Globalization* (Cambridge, Mass.: MIT Press, 2009), 70, 71.

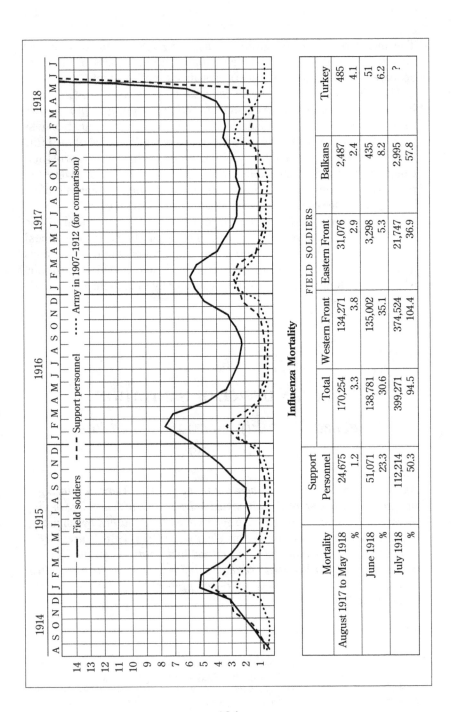

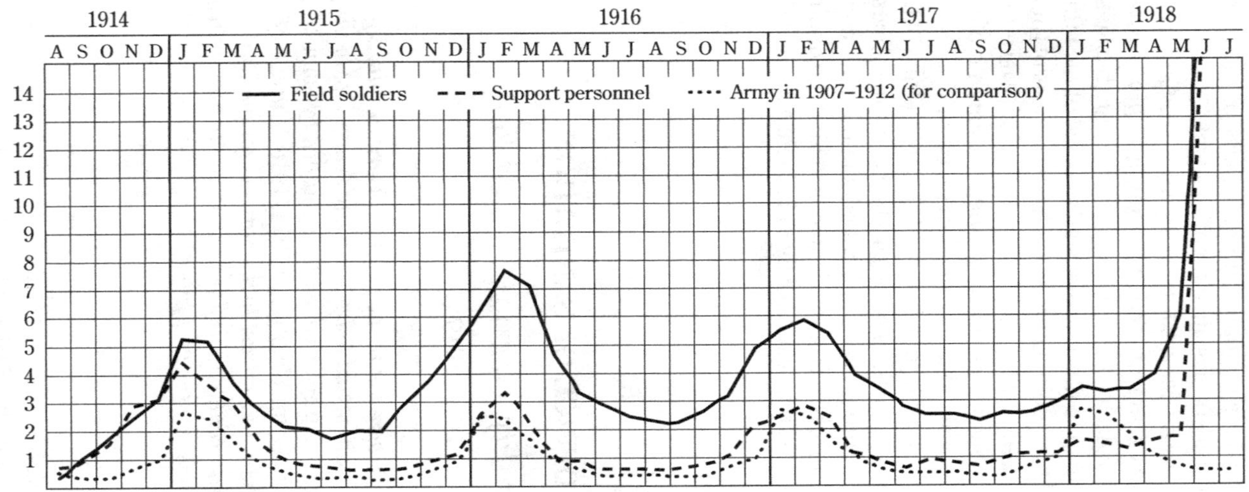

Influenza Mortality

Mortality	Support Personnel	FIELD SOLDIERS Total	Western Front	Eastern Front	Balkans	Turkey
August 1917 to May 1918	24,675	170,254	134,271	31,076	2,487	485
%	1.2	3.3	3.8	2.9	2.4	4.1
June 1918	51,071	138,781	135,002	3,298	435	51
%	23.3	30.6	35.1	5.3	8.2	6.2
July 1918	112,214	399,271	374,524	21,747	2,995	?
%	50.3	94.5	104.4	36.9	57.8	

52

THE TIMES (LONDON)

Awaiting the Enemy Attack

July 12, 1918

In this selection, the reporter for The Times *of London notes the incidence of influenza among German troops and speculates that it might explain the failure of the German army to continue its assault during the Spring Offensive.*

The front as a whole is so quiet that it almost seems to have relapsed into the conditions of stationary warfare again, though it is incredible that the Germans can afford to allow it to do so, and we are well aware of enemy preparedness for attack on various sectors. . . .

The question how far influenza is responsible for the present enemy inactivity is an interesting speculation, so long as we do not allow ourselves to attach too great importance to it. That it is extraordinarily widespread, we know, and we get frequent evidence of the virulence of the disease in individual units in the front line. Thus, one company of the 61st Regiment is so prostrated that it had to be relieved. Two whole battalions of the 232nd Regiment were so reduced that they had to be withdrawn from the line; one company of the 68th Reserve Regiment shrank to a fighting strength of 42 men instead of the normal 120; one company of the 174th Regiment was similarly reduced to 17 men; the whole of the 187th Division had to be taken out of the line because it had ceased to be effective; and another division, the 119th, could not be relieved because the relieving troops were incapable of coming in. Whether the aggregate effects of the epidemic are really enough to interfere with the general plans of the enemy or not, the subject is at least interesting.

"Awaiting the Enemy Attack," *The Times* (London), July 12, 1918, 6.

53

DAILY EXPRESS (LONDON)

New Attack in the North?

July 18, 1918

The correspondent for London's Daily Express *suggests that the inability of the German army to take advantage of its gains during the early stages of the Spring Offensive was owing to the condition of its troops, who were struck hard by the flu.*

The enemy's aggressiveness has been confined this week to heavy bursts of artillery fire. His batteries were very energetic during the night around Ypres and against the Allied trenches defending the Flemish hills. The infantry, however, is apparently too weak or dispirited to give any exhibitions of hostility, and is content to hold its defences. . . .

Some of these divisions have been depleted by illness, and convalescents from the "influenza camps" are only just beginning to return in large numbers. In spite of this epidemic, which has been specially severe in the 4th and 6th German Armies, north of La Bassée, a vast amount of constructional work has been carried out behind their front. . . .

Nor has the prevalence of influenza in Belgium been allowed to interfere with the intensive field training on a large scale.

"New Attack in the North?" *Daily Express* (London), July 18, 1918, 1.

54

C. W. VINING

Treatment of Influenza

November 30, 1918

Efforts to combat the flu were hampered by the lack of any central coordinating body in many countries of the world. In this letter to The Lancet, *a British physician laments the situation he and his colleagues encountered, although it must be pointed out that the United States, which did possess both state and national public health agencies, suffered particularly heavily from the flu, both in morbidity and mortality.*

To the Editor of *The Lancet*

Sir,—

. . . The civilian population has suffered severely, not so much because we have been unable to make up our minds as to the actual causative agent of the disease, or whether one should administer a dose of 10 million or 500 million dead influenza bacilli, or even because we have been unable to provide a definitely curative agent against the virus, but rather owing to the distress and misery caused by the apparent helplessness of the public health, Poor-law, and hospital authorities to do anything adequate to deal with a situation where nursing and care of acutely ill people have been an urgent need.

The difficulties, of course, have been great, but failure to cope with the problem has obviously been due to want of organisation rather than of beds, doctors, and nurses. The war has clearly demonstrated that in the hands of a central authority organisation can overcome everything, and the medical and nursing professions have been able to successfully meet situations of unparalleled difficulty. In one way, therefore, the epidemic has done good. It has proved the urgent need for an efficient State Medical Authority. The existence of such an authority would have made it possible for a clear-cut line of campaign to have been immediately instituted. It would have been possible for that authority to have at once ordered the closing of every hospital and infirmary bed to all but

---

C. W. Vining, "Treatment of Influenza," *The Lancet*, November 30, 1918, 757.

urgent cases. In this way wards could have been set apart and nurses set free for the care of large numbers of influenzal pneumonia. Under such conditions it would have been reasonably possible to attempt to carry out . . . excellent principles of treatment and so give the patients a better chance, and at the same time to have saved many families from the distress and misery produced by attempting to look after acutely ill relatives under conditions that are all against recovery.

55

THE UNION OF SOUTH AFRICA

Bill to Make Provision for the Public Health

January 6, 1919

In South Africa, the experience of the influenza pandemic provided a great deal of impetus toward the creation of a national Department of Public Health. Previous efforts to consolidate public health measures had always run up against the decentralized nature of the Union, comprised as it was of a number of states that sought to go their own way. This bill overrode those objections and established a centralized agency. Despite its neutral language, the bill's provisions concerned only whites; by excluding Africans and by removing poor whites from the urban slums, the act helped to bring about racial residential segregation in the cities of South Africa.

Be it enacted by the King's Most Excellent Majesty, the Senate and the House of Assembly of the Union of South Africa, as follows:— . . .

2. There shall be for the Union a department, to be known as the department of Public Health, which shall be under the control of a Minister and in respect of which there shall be a portfolio of Public Health.

3. (1) The functions of the department of Public Health shall, subject to the provisions of this Act, be to prevent, or safeguard against,

"Bill to Make Provision for the Public Health," The Union of South Africa, *Government Gazette Extraordinary* XXXV, no. 938, January 6, 1919.

the introduction of infectious disease into the Union from outside, to promote the public health and the prevention, limitation or suppression of infectious, communicable or preventable diseases within the Union, to advise and assist provincial administrations and local authorities in regard to matters affecting the public health; to promote or carry out researches and investigations in connection with the prevention or treatment of human diseases; to prepare and publish reports and statistical or other information relative to the public health, and generally to carry out in accordance with directions the powers and duties in relation to the public health conferred or imposed on the Governor-General or the Minister by this Act or otherwise.

56

SOUTH AFRICAN MEDICAL RECORD

New Public Health Bill

January 11, 1919

The South African professional medical community gave its enthusiastic approval to the creation of a new department of public health.

We have received a copy of the draft of this Bill. It is, as must be the case, a most voluminous measure, and the task of piloting it through Parliament will be an extremely difficult one. A consolidating measure on Public Health has been, ever since Union, one of the most crying necessities of the country. . . . One realises how utterly chaotic and absurd the present position is. But the task of consolidation is an extremely difficult one, owing to the multiplicity of competing interests, rural and urban, Government, Provincial and local, all desiring to have untrammelled powers of control and expenditure, combined with the right of calling upon someone else to foot the bill. . . .

Public Health, if this Bill passes without material mutilation, will become, from A to Z, a Union responsibility as regards control and very

"New Public Health Bill," *South African Medical Record,* January 11, 1919, 1–3.

largely one as regards finance. We are bound to record our opinion that this is the only course likely to lead to an effective Public Health administration. We are as much alive to the advantages of devolution as anyone. . . . But we recognise that Public Health is just one of those things which, in a country so thinly populated as this, must be centralised. . . . There are two sound medical reasons why devolution is impossible. One is that disease does not respect artificial political boundaries. The other is that constituting the Union Government the administrative unit affords the only hope of forming a Public Health medical service sufficiently strong and sufficiently elastic to cope successfully, from the technical side, with the problems of Public Health. . . . We venture to lay special stress upon this word "elastic," in the light of the lessons so painfully taught us in the recent epidemic. . . .

We therefore welcome the general spirit of the Bill; and we see very little indeed to criticize in its details. They are sweeping, and thorough to a degree, and have been apparently conceived with an eye to one thing, and one thing only—efficiency. That the Bill will meet with much opposition . . . we have no doubt, but we indulge the hope that the fact of the recent influenza epidemic being still fresh in the memories of our legislators of the more obtuse type will give it a better chance of passage without material mutilation than would have been the case otherwise.

57

SIERRA LEONE WEEKLY NEWS

The Health of Freetown

September 21, 1918

The Sierra Leone Weekly News *was founded in 1884 by Joseph C. May and Edward W. Blyden, Western-educated Sierra Leonean elites who turned it into one of the most influential papers in West Africa. It used the columns of its editorial page to lambast British colonial authorities for their indifference to the effects of the flu on the African population.*

"The Health of Freetown," *Sierra Leone Weekly News*, September 21, 1918, 8.

Another fact of the epidemic is a revelation of the kind of feeling which is at present entertained by local whites to local blacks. Nobody who knew and lived in Sierra Leone thirty or forty years ago but must have perceived the great difference in interest which the epidemic has brought to the surface among our rulers. In days gone by Freetown would have been divided into sections, and all qualified Doctors, whether black or white, would have been put on service. The Principal Medical Officer himself would have been seen amongst people at the Grassfields [area outside Freetown where native Sierra Leoneans lived] giving instructions; the trees would have been trimmed; the conditions of the air would have been tested; and . . . so the present epidemic would have been made an instrument of enlarged knowledge of the sanitary condition of the country. But why was there such a remarkable coldness amounting to indifference in our rulers with respect to ourselves? Feeling appears to have been changed; the imperialism of the twentieth century being at the bottom. . . .

The epidemic ought therefore to be made a distinct point of departure in the history of our country. . . . Our welfare lies in our standing up and doing things for ourselves. We have reached a stage where we can take care of ourselves in several things.

58

LAGOS STANDARD

Failure of British Authorities

October 2, 1918

In this editorial, the owner of the Lagos Standard *articulates the opinion of many educated Nigerians that British colonial officials during the influenza pandemic not only failed in their responsibilities to ensure the well-being of their subjects, but actively discriminated against Africans.*

Editorial: "Influenza in Lagos," *Lagos Standard,* October 2, 1918.

It is not too late even now to adopt methods that will help the people and encourage them to have confidence in the efforts of the Authorities to guard their health. It is not a wise thing to depend on Force as the most essential weapon for stamping out an epidemic. The co-operation of the people with the work of the Sanitary Authorities is very essential and that co-operation cannot be secured by the present methods of the Sanitary Authorities which make the people run away not from dread of the disease but from fear of sanitary officials and their ways. You close up churches whilst the very public office in which the very first case of Influenza in the town occurred remains open till this day, and other public offices like the Law Courts, the Printing Office, the Secretariat where large numbers of people congregate daily are not closed. You provide isolation and observation accomodation [*sic*] for natives inadequate at best and unsuitable in many particulars some four or five miles outside the town and compel them to live under conditions which they consider are injurious to their health, and for your own people you provide wards in the General Hospital in town under the best of condition. You cannot stamp out an epidemic by the passing of ordinances and the rigid enforcement of regulations which are impracticable. The last few days have shown that the Authorities have no adequate provision either of medical staff or hospitals accomodation for the isolation and observation of illness in an epidemic of Influenza in a town of 80,000 persons. Our advice to the Sanitary Authorities is Make Haste Slowly.

59

BUCHI EMECHETA

The Slave Girl

1977

African historians rely heavily upon oral tradition to provide the sources for their histories, as written materials for so much of the past simply do not exist. In The Slave Girl, *Buchi Emecheta (b.1944) tells the story of her mother's experiences with the influenza pandemic, the account of which she learned from her mother as a young child. The novel places the*

Buchi Emecheta, *The Slave Girl* (New York: George Braziller, 1980), pp. 25–29.

flu, thought to have been brought to Nigeria by white men, at the heart of the story, which includes an account of a Women's War fought by Nigerian women against colonial authority. In The Slave Girl, *Emecheta's mother, named here Ojebeta, is orphaned by the flu and is sold by her brother into slavery.*

"*Pom*! *Pom*! *Pom*! The rumours that have been going around are true. *Pom*! There is a kind of death coming from across the salty waters. It has killed many people in Isele Azagba, it is creeping to Ogwashi, it is now coming to us. They call it Felenza. It is white man's death. They shoot it into the air, and we breathe it in and die. *Pom*! *Pom*. . . ."

People, some on the verge of eating their evening meal, some still thudding their yam for the meal in their wooden mortars, listened helplessly as the gongman went round Ibuza with his unwelcome news. . . . Everybody felt a kind of chill; not that an epidemic was anything new to the people of Ibuza, but at least previously they had always known what measures to take to avert mass disaster. They had experienced diseases like smallpox. . . . They knew that to stop it spreading throughout the villages any victim had to be isolated, so when somebody was attacked he would be taken into the bush and left there to die. . . .

But this felenza was a new thing that the "Potokis" [Portuguese] had shot into the air, though everyone wondered why. . . . The people of Ibuza pondered, speculated and hoped that it would never come to them, for where were they to run to?

But soon it came to Ogwashi, and within days men started dropping down dead on their farms. Death was always so sudden that the relatives were too shocked to cry.

Ojebeta's father, the strong man Okwuekwu Oda, was one of the first to be hit. She remembered that morning he had come to where she was still sleeping by the wood fire. . . . As she watched her mother fill his pipe for him and light it she heard her say:

"If the head is so bad, stay at home today."

Her father had snapped: "Cowards fear death. It can catch up with you anywhere, whether you're lying down on your sleeping mat or digging in your farm. I don't want to die lying down like a crochety old man. I am going to the farm. Besides, who told you headaches mean felenza?"

With that he stalked out puffing angrily at his pipe as he went, smoke from the pipe following him like a line of mist.

That was the last time Ojebeta saw her father on his feet; she could still hear his footfall as he marched away in indignation. He came back in the evening, but carried by some people. He had died. Felenza had killed him on his farm.

After that it seemed to Ojebeta's young mind that the whole world was dying, one by one. Her father's hut was pulled to the ground and a mourning hut was quickly constructed for her mother. . . . When felenza was at its height her eldest brother decided to leave home in search of a European job; he would rather go and face whatever fate awaited him in an unknown place than stay in Ibuza waiting for felenza to come to him. . . .

Although Ojebeta never heard her mother complain of any headaches, as her father had, she had become very aware of Death—that somebody who could take away your loved ones with little warning. . . . One morning . . . Ojebeta called out to her [mother] in the gentle tone she found herself using recently, since her father's death. Something of her, she did not know what, seemed to have been buried with him. . . . She called gently again and when there was no response guessed that her mother was still asleep. It was no wonder her mother slept late these days, for there was nowhere for her to go, no kernels for her to press to make oil, no cassava for her to fetch. She was confined to her hut like a prisoner until her months of mourning were over. Maybe after that, things would go back to being almost as they used to be before the arrival of that horrible gas that took her dear father away. Ojebeta snuggled closer to the nipple of her mother's sagging breast. The wind went on and on, but she was no longer frightened. Her mother was there by her, so no harm could come to her now. She fell asleep.

She was startled by a voice wailing and shouting as if hell had been let loose. Then a strong pair of hands was lifting her from the mud floor on which she was lying beside her mother. The hands were those of her brother Okolie, and he too was crying. So was her mother's friend Ozubu. . . . They were crying and shaking their heads. The loud noises they were making had attracted near neighbours and relatives. Her father's sister, who normally was not on speaking terms with her mother, was now leading Ojebeta away from her brother, at the same time reminding them all that they were not supposed to make so much noise while the present trouble was still about. She was not herself being very successful in this, however, for she was crying too.

By now Ojebeta understood. Her mother Umeadi had gone too, had been taken away from her by the same felenza.

60

YOUNG INDIA

Famine and Grip Sweeping India

February 1919

Young India *was the official organ of India's Congress Party, run by Mohandas K. Gandhi (1869–1948). In its pages, Congress Party members blame British officials for the severity of the famine and illness that stalked India.*

The country is face to face with famine and has suffered very heavily from the influenza epidemic. It seems that one more scourge has been added to the long list of diseases which have been ravaging the country for so many years—malaria, cholera, plague—and now influenza. Influenza has been rampant, perhaps all over the world, for the past several months, but we fear that nowhere else has it claimed so many victims as in India. . . . If the estimate given by the correspondent of the Times is correct, then . . . of the population throughout India the total death roll would be . . . from 15 to 30 millions. . . . The chief cause of heavy mortality in India from all kinds of diseases is the low vitality of the people, the direct outcome of insufficient food—a cause from which about 100 millions of the population, at least, suffer, even in prosperous years.

"Famine and Grip Sweeping India," *Young India*, Vol. II, no. 2, February 1919, 41.

61

YOUNG INDIA

Editorial Notes and News

May 1919

These articles appeared in Young India *in the exact order as laid out below. The riots provoked a deadly response by the British that came to be called the Amritsar Massacre, which marks the moment when Indian nationalists ceased to agitate for mere self-governance within the British Empire and sought out-and-out independence from Britain.*

6,000,000 Deaths

The Secretary for India states that he has received the following telegram from the Government of India with regard to the recent outbreaks of influenza and cholera at Bombay and in other parts of India. . . .

Deaths from influenza in India as a whole in 1918 are calculated at 5,000,000 for British India and 1,000,000 for Indian States.

Famine

The Manchester *Guardian* publishes the following letter which speaks for itself:

> The crop failure in India is perhaps the most extensive on record. . . . These incredibly high prices, matched also by the dearness of clothing, fuel, and other necessaries, and by the non-existence of fodder for more than a small proportion of the cattle have followed on the top of outbreaks of influenza, which in some places swept away as much as one-sixth or even one-fifth of the population in a couple of months. . . .

"Editorial Notes and News," in *Young India,* Vol. II, no. 5, May 1919, 99–102.

Riots in India

From the New York *Times* we print the following: . . .

> Widespread disturbances in India were referred to in Parliament tonight as being the outcome of what was described as the "passive resistance" movement against the recent Indian legislation known as the Rowlatt act, intended to combat seditious conspiracy.
>
> The movement originated with the home rule element in Bombay and has taken shape in attacks on officials and Europeans and on property.
>
> . . . There have been disturbances recently at Lahore and a few casualties at Amritsar, thirty-three miles eastward, where three bank managers were burned to death in the Town Hall, two banks destroyed, the telegraph office wrecked, and three Europeans killed. At Ahmedabad a mob attacked and burned the telegraph office and two Government buildings. Here, also, there were a few casualties.
>
> There have been disorders in which some persons have been wounded at Bombay, but, the statement says, in most of these places military forces are now maintaining order.

62

CARY T. GRAYSON

Statement about Wilson's Health at the Paris Peace Conference

1960

Admiral Cary Grayson (1878–1938) was Woodrow Wilson's (1856–1924) personal physician and had attended the president throughout his years in office, establishing a regime of diet, exercise, and rest that helped keep Wilson fit. Grayson feared that the rigors of the Paris Peace Conference would undermine Wilson's level of health, which had been achieved by such extensive effort.

Cary T. Grayson, *Woodrow Wilson: An Intimate Memoir* (New York: Holt, Rinehart and Winston, 1960), 82, 85.

I dreaded the added strain of his [Wilson's] personal attendance upon the Peace Conference. I foresaw that he would be in almost daily contest with antagonists. I knew that he would see sights which would drain his emotions, and I feared that in a new environment it would be impossible for him to maintain the systematic habits of life which had sustained him at home even during the struggle of war. There was something else which I did not foresee, an attack of influenza in Paris, which proved to be one of the contributory causes of his final breakdown. . . .

In the early spring of 1919 came that ill-omened attack of influenza, the insidious effects of which he was not in good condition to resist. Then followed asthma, which broke the sleep that had always been his sheet anchor. In the pressure of public business or private grief he had always been able to sleep, but now asthmatic coughing woke him at intervals all through the night. He was less obedient than he had been to his physician's advice. He insisted on holding conferences while he was still confined to his sickbed. When he was able to get up he began to drive himself as hard as before—morning, afternoon, and frequently evening conferences.

63

IRWIN HOOD HOOVER

The Truth about Wilson's Illness

1934

Irwin (Ike) Hoover (1871–1933) served as a butler in the White House for more than forty years. He attended Wilson while in Paris during the peace talks and recorded his observations of his employer's state of health in a 1934 memoir.

In Europe there were trying times for him. It was so different from what he had been passing through the previous five or six years. Now he was

From Irwin Hood (Ike) Hoover, *Forty-Two Years in the White House* (Boston: Houghton Mifflin, 1934), 98–99.

certainly the whole show—at the beginning at least. The responsibility seemed tremendous. I was by his side for twelve or fourteen hours every day. My hours were his hours. There was not a let-up, all days were alike. He was so intent that it was a positive burden to try to keep up with him. The others of us in the party wanted to see Europe and especially Paris, but our opportunities were limited on account of the intensity and concentration of the President. But the day came when he wavered. The load was too much. Some saw it from one angle, some from another. He went to bed ostensibly with a cold. When he got on his feet again he was a different man.

Even while lying in bed he manifested peculiarities, one of which was to limit the use of all the automobiles to strictly official purposes, when previously he had been so liberal in his suggestions that his immediate party should have the benefit of this possible diversion, in view of the long hours we were working. When he got back on the job, his peculiar ideas were even more pronounced. He now became obsessed with the idea that every French employee about the place was a spy for the French Government. Nothing we could say could disabuse his mind of this thought. He insisted they all understood English, when, as a matter of fact, there was just one of them among the two dozen or more who understood a single word of English. About this time he also acquired the peculiar notion that he was responsible for all the property in the furnished palace he was occupying. He raised quite a fuss on two occasions when he noticed articles of furniture had been removed. Upon investigation—for no one else noticed the change—it was learned that the custodian of the property for the French owner had seen fit to do a little rearranging. Coming from the President, whom we all knew so well, these were very funny things, and we could but surmise that something queer was happening in his mind.

One thing was certain: he was never the same after this little spell of illness.

64

HERBERT HOOVER

Wilson at the Paris Peace Conference

1942

Herbert Hoover (1874–1964, no relation to Ike Hoover), who eventually became chief executive himself, served as a member of the United States delegation to the Paris Peace Conference, and saw firsthand the toll the flu took on his president.

During the Peace Conference, he [Wilson] was out of action for some time, announced as influenza. When he came out, he was drawn, exhausted, and haggard. He sometimes groped for ideas. His mind constantly strove for previous decisions and precedents in even minor matters. He clung to them.

Prior to that time, in all matters with which I had to deal, he was incisive, quick to grasp essentials, unhesitating in conclusions, and most willing to take advice from men he trusted. After the time I mention, others as well as I found we had to push against an unwilling mind. And at times, when I just had to get decisions, I suffered as much from the necessity to mentally push as he did in coming to conclusions. Ike Hoover, who was his servant, told me in later years that Wilson had at that time his first stroke of thrombosis. Ike was a most unreliable reporter. If this be correct, however, it explains much subsequent history. . . .

On Saturday, June twenty-eighth, we all went to the Hall of Mirrors at Versailles to witness the signing. . . . I had difficulty in keeping my mind on the ceremony. It was constantly traveling along the fearful consequences of many paragraphs which these men were signing with such pomp, and their effect on millions of human beings; then moving back to the high hopes with which I had landed in Europe eight months before. And I came away depressed and not exultant.

From Herbert Hoover, *America's First Crusade* (New York: Scribner's, 1942), 64–66.

A Chronology of the Influenza Pandemic and Related Events (1918–1929)

1918 *January 8* Woodrow Wilson delivers speech to U.S. Congress outlining his Fourteen Points for peace.

January–February Influenza appears in Kansas.

March–April First wave of disease. Influenza spreads to southern U.S. states, and then to Europe aboard troopships.

March Germans begin Spring Offensive against Allies on the western front.

May Influenza appears in Europe. German offensive stalls.

June–July Influenza strikes German army with great force. German offensive fails.

August–September Second wave of disease. New strain of influenza appears in France, Boston, and Sierra Leone in Africa, spreading thence to Asia and the Pacific Islands, devastating populations everywhere.

October–November Height of mortality owing to influenza. German retreat.

November 11 Armistice brings World War I to an end.

1919 *February* Third wave of influenza outbreak takes place.

February–June Peace talks take place in Paris. David Lloyd George and Georges Clemenceau fall ill to influenza.

April 3 Woodrow Wilson contracts influenza.

April 10 Rioting in the Punjab province, India.

April 13 Amritsar massacre in Punjab province, India.

June 28 Germans sign Treaty of Versailles.

1929 *December* Women's War in southeastern Nigeria.

Questions for Consideration

1. In what ways did the 1918–1919 influenza strain differ from other influenzas? How many waves did the epidemic comprise, and how did they differ?
2. How did wartime restrictions on the flow of information out of Allied and Central Powers countries affect global perceptions of the flu?
3. By what means did the flu spread so rapidly? What social, political, and economic factors played roles in its spread, both locally and around the world?
4. What physical symptoms did flu sufferers present? What kind of mental, emotional, and psychological impact did the flu have on its victims?
5. What treatments did physicians prescribe to address the flu? What do these treatments tell us about the nature of medical and scientific knowledge in 1919? What treatments did traditional medicine offer in countries such as China and Japan? How were those similar to or different from the treatments prescribed in the West? How did Western doctors react to these traditional remedies? What does that say about Western attitudes to non-Western traditions?
6. How did public officials respond to the pandemic in various cities and countries? How did the pandemic change expectations of governments' role in protecting and maintaining public health?
7. Were the official guidelines for treating the flu provided by various governments (Documents 28, 30, and 32–35) helpful to patients and public health? How did they differ from the advice offered by doctors and laypeople in various letters and newspaper accounts (Documents 36, 37, and 38)?
8. Do perceptions of the flu and treatment prescriptions appear to have changed over time? How do doctors' characterizations and reactions to the illness evolve over the course of the pandemic?
9. Compare recollections of the flu written by survivors and memoirists years later (such as Documents 10 and 48) with accounts taken during the height of the epidemic (Documents 7, 8, and 9). In what ways are they consistent? How do they differ?

10. Why do you think that some countries were hit harder by the flu, in terms of mortality, than others? Within countries, why were some ethnic groups hit harder than others?
11. What challenges do historians face in assessing the flu's impact on World War I? Is it really possible to know how much of an effect the flu may have had on the outcome of the war?
12. Given what the scientific community has learned about the influenza of 1918–1919 in the years since, what is there to learn from reading the medical community's perceptions of it at the time? Why do the perspectives of period physicians matter if they've been proven wrong in the decades since?
13. What role did the influenza pandemic serve in stimulating anticolonial feelings among colonized peoples? How did this role differ in various colonies?
14. Compare accounts of President Woodrow Wilson's health at the Versailles Conference (Documents 62–64) with descriptions of flu symptoms described in Documents 12 and 13. Might Wilson's health have contributed to his inability to obtain a peace based on his Fourteen Points? Might the flu have had an influence on Germany's agreement to the Treaty of Versailles as well?
15. Did it surprise you to learn that the pandemic killed more people worldwide than died in World War I? If so, why did you know so little about such a catastrophic event? Why did the war and other world events that followed eclipse the ravages of the pandemic in collective memory? How did memories of this experience differ between Western and non-Western countries?

Selected Bibliography

Barry, John. *The Great Influenza.* New York: Viking, 2004.

Byerly, Carol R. *Fever of War: The Influenza Epidemic in the U.S. Army during World War I.* New York: New York University Press, 2005.

Collier, Richard. *The Plague of the Spanish Lady.* New York: Atheneum, 1974.

Crosby, Alfred. *America's Forgotten Pandemic: The Influenza of 1918.* Cambridge, U.K.: Cambridge University Press, 1989.

Emecheta, Buchi. *The Slave Girl.* New York: George Braziller, 1977.

Honigsbaum, Mark. *Living with Enza: The Forgotten Story of Britain and the Great Flu Pandemic of 1918.* New York: Palgrave Macmillan, 2008.

Johnson, Niall. *Britain and the 1918–19 Influenza Pandemic: A Dark Epilogue.* London: Routledge, 2006.

Kent, Susan Kingsley. *Aftershocks: Politics and Trauma in Britain, 1918–1931.* Basingstoke, U.K.: Palgrave Macmillan, 2009.

Kolata, Gina. *Flu: The Story of the Great Influenza Pandemic of 1918 and the Search for the Virus that Caused It.* New York: Farrar, Straus and Giroux, 1999.

MacMillan, Margaret. *Paris 1919.* New York: Random House, 2001.

Matera, Marc, Misty L. Bastian, and Susan Kingsley Kent. *The Women's War of 1929: Gender and Violence in Colonial Nigeria.* Basingstoke, U.K.: Palgrave Macmillan, 2011.

"The 1918–1919 Influenza Pandemic in the United States," *Public Health Reports* 125, supplement 3 (April 2010): 3–144.

Phillips, Howard, and David Killingray, eds., *The Spanish Influenza Pandemic of 1918–19: New Perspectives.* London: Routledge, 2003.

Price-Smith, Andrew. *Contagion and Chaos: Disease, Ecology, and National Security in the Era of Globalization.* Cambridge, Mass.: MIT Press, 2009.

Acknowledgments (*continued from p. ii*)

Figure 1. Taubenberger, Jeffery K., and David M. Morens. "1918 Influenza: The Mother of All Pandemics." *Emerging Infectious Diseases* 12.1 (2006): 15-22, Figure 2. *PMC.*

Photo, p. 12. SPL/Photo Researchers, Inc.

Document 9. Edwina Palmer and Geoffrey W. Rice. A Japanese physician's response to pandemic influenza: Ijiro Gomibuchi and the "Spanish flu" in Yaita-Ch, 1918–1919. *Bulletin of the History of Medicine* 66:4 (1992), 569–70, 573. © 1992 The Johns Hopkins University Press. Reprinted with permission of The Johns Hopkins University Press.

Document 10. Rachel Wedeking interview with Josie Brown, in "A Winding Sheet and a Wooden Box," *Navy Medicine* 77, No. 3 (May–June 1986): 18–19.

Document 38. Image courtesy of The Advertising Archives.

Document 41. Translated by Mary K. Long, May 2011.

Document 49. Excerpts from "Yonder Peasant, Who Is He?" in *Memories of a Catholic Girlhood,* copyright © 1948 and renewed 1975 by Mary McCarthy, reprinted with permission by Houghton Mifflin Harcourt Publishing Company.

Document 59. Buchi Emecheta, *The Slave Girl* (New York: George Braziller, 1980), 25–29. Reprinted with the permission of George Braziller, Inc.

Document 62. Cary T. Grayson, *Woodrow Wilson: An Intimate Memoir* (New York: Holt, Rinehart and Winston, 1960), 82, 85.

Document 63. Excerpt from *Forty-Two Years in the White House* by Irwin Hood Hoover. Copyright © 1934 by James Osborne Hoover and Mildred Hoover Stewart. Copyright © renewed 1961 by James Osborne Hoover. Reprinted by permission of Houghton Mifflin Harcourt Publishing Company. All rights reserved.

Document 64. Courtesy Herbert Hoover Foundation, Inc.

Index